HOSANNA!

A NATIONAL LITURGICAL SONGBOOK FOR IRELAND

GENERAL EDITOR: PAUL KENNY

 the columba press

the columba press

8 Lr Kilmacud Road,
Blackrock, Co Dublin.

First edition 1987
Designed by Bill Bolger
Typeset by Typeform Ltd., Dublin
Printed in Ireland by
Mount Salus Press, Dublin.

ISBN: 0 948183 45 4

Sole distributors in Northern Ireland:
DRC BOOKSHOPS
22/24 Fleetwood Street
Belfast BT14 6AX

The editor and the publishers thank the following for permission to use material in their copyright:

Archdiocesan Music Office, Philadelphia (No 49); Geoffrey Chapman Ltd, London (Nos 29,34,42,90, 108,114,124,157,158,159,167); Epoch Universal Publications, Arizona (No 138); Franciscan Communications, Los Angeles (No 88); G.I.A. Publications, Chicago (Nos 65,89); Michael Hodgetts, Sutton Coldfield (54); Brian Kelly CSSp, Dublin (No 33); McCrimmon Publishing Co Ltd, Great Wakering (No 68,86); Mgr John Moloney, Dublin (Nos 38,137,142); The Lady Abbess of Stanbrook Abbey, Worcester (No 103); Sister Pamela Stotter, Birr (No 30); A. P. Watt Ltd, London for Grail Psalms 4,15,22,32,39,41, 42,84,118,129. Weston Priory, Vermont (Nos 41,154); Word of God Music, Ann Arbor (No 148); World Library Publications, Chicago (Nos 5,6,9,10,19,52,55,62,73, 76,87,96,116,117,120,171,172,173). Rev William Jabusch, Mundelein, USA (No 168); Gethsemane Abbey, Kentucky (No 101); Oxford University Press (Nos 84,99); Trustees of Clifford Howell SJ, London (No 133); St Louis Priory, Missouri (No 143); The Living Parish Series, Sydney (No 67); Roger Ruston, OP (No 37); David Higham Assoc. Ltd (94). Bishop Donal Murray (35,66,144,155,165); Aideen O'Sullivan (No 24); Sr Margaret Daly (No 79); J Fennelly (No 31, . 107). The Estate of Seán Ó Riada (174); Mary Kelly (175).

English translation of the Order of Mass and music from the Roman Missal, © 1969, 1971, International Committee on English in the Liturgy, Inc. All rights reserved.

Acknowledgement is due to the International Consultation on English Texts for the Gloria, Nicene Creed, Apostles' Creed, Sanctus and Dialogue before the Preface.

Ord an Aifrinn © 1969 Institiúid Chumarsáide Chaitliceach na hÉireann.

We have made every effort to trace all known copyright material. If we have inadvertently used any copyright material without permission, we offer our apologies and invite the copyright holders to contact us so that the error can be rectified.

CONTENTS

NB: *Titles beginning with "The" are found under 'T'*

The references in square brackets are to accompaniments. V = *The Veritas Hymnal*; AA = *Alleluia! Amen!*; 20C = *The 20th Century Folk Hymnal.*

INDEX OF FIRST LINES

Priestly people, kingly people, holy people (120)
Promised Lord and Christ is he (37)

Receive O Father in thy love (125)
Regina caeli, laetare, alleluia (123)
Remember those O Lord (124)
Rorate caeli (126)

Salve Regina, mater misericordiae (127)
Sancti venite, corpus Christi sumite (128)
'Sé an Tiarna m'aoire (131)
See amid the winter's snow (130)
See how the rose of Judah (132)
See us, Lord, about thine altar (133)
'Sé Íosa an fíréan (13)
Show us Lord, the path of life (129)
Show us, Lord, your mercy (135)
Silent night, holy night (134)
Sing praise to our creator (136)
Sing praise to the Lord all our days (137)
Sing to the Lord, alleluia (138)
Síormholadh is glóir duit, a Athair shíoraí (139)
Soul of my saviour, sanctify my breast (140)
Stabat mater dolorosa (141)
Star of sea and ocean (143)
Stay with us Lord, we pray you, alleluia (142)
Sweet sacrament divine (144)

Tantum ergo sacramentum (145)
The bells of the angelus (146)
The church's one foundation (147)
The day thou gavest, Lord, is ended (149)
The first nowell the angel did say (151)
The king of love my shepherd is (150)
The light of Christ has come into the world (148)
The Lord is my shepherd (152)
The Lord Jesus, after eating with his friends (154)
The Lord made known to Israel (155)
The Lord's my shepherd, I'll not want (153)
Therefore we before him bending (156)
The seed is Christ's, the harvest his (157)
This day God gives me (158)

This is my will, my one command (159)
To Christ, the prince of peace (160)
To Jesus Christ our sov'reign king (161)
To thee, O heart of Jesus (162)

Ubi caritas est vera, Deus ibi est (164)

Veni, Creator Spiritus (163)

We praise you and thank you, our Father above (165)
We praise you, God, confessing you as Lord! (167)
We three kings of orient are (166)
Whatsoever you do to the least of my brothers (168)
When I behold the wondrous cross (169)
While shepherds watched their flocks by night (170)
Without seeing you, we love you (171)

Yes, I shall arise and return to my father (172)
You are the honour (173)
You satisfy the hungry heart with gift of finest wheat (49)

THE ORDER OF MASS

THE INTRODUCTORY RITES

The Mass may begin with the singing or recitation of the Entrance Antiphon *or a* Hymn *whilst the celebrant and servers approach the altar. The people stand.*

Celebrant: In the name of the Father, and of the Son, and of the Holy Spirit.
People: **Amen.**

One of the following greetings is used:
1.
C. The grace of our Lord Jesus Christ and the love of God
and the fellowship of the Holy Spirit be with you all.
P. **And also with you.**
2.
C. The grace and peace of God our Father and the Lord Jesus Christ be with you.
P. **Blessed be God, the Father of our Lord Jesus Christ.**
Or **And also with you.**
3.
C. The Lord be with you.
P. **And also with you.**

THE PENITENTIAL RITE

The celebrant invites the people to repent of their sins using one of the following forms:
1.
C. My brothers and sisters (*or similar wording*), to prepare ourselves to celebrate the sacred mysteries,
let us call to mind our sins.
After a brief silence all say:
**I confess to almighty God,
and to you, my brothers and sisters,
that I have sinned
through my own fault** (*all strike their breast*)
**in my thoughts and in my words,
in what I have done,**

**and in what I have failed to do;
and I ask blessed Mary, ever virgin,
all the angels and saints,
and you, my brothers and sisters,
to pray for me to the Lord our God.**
2.
C. My brothers and sisters (*or similar wording*), to prepare ourselves to celebrate the sacred mysteries,
let us call to mind our sins.
After a brief silence, the celebrant says:
Lord we have sinned against you: Lord, have mercy.
P. **Lord, have mercy.**
C. Lord, show us your mercy and love.
P. **And grant us your salvation.**
3.
C. My brothers and sisters (*or similar wording*), to prepare ourselves to celebrate the sacred mysteries,
Let us call to mind our sins.
After a brief silence the celebrant says the following, or similar words. The people's response, however, remains the same.
You were sent to heal the contrite: Lord, have mercy.
P. **Lord, have mercy.**
C. You came to call sinners: Christ, have mercy.
P. **Christ, have mercy.**
C. You plead for us at the right hand of the Father:
Lord, have mercy.
P. **Lord, have mercy.**

The Act of Penance *is followed by the* Absolution.
C. May almighty God have mercy on us, forgive us our sins,
and bring us to everlasting life.
P. **Amen.**

The Kyrie eleison *now follows unless it has already been used in one of the forms of the* Act of Penance.
C. Lord, have mercy.
P. **Lord, have mercy.**
C. Christ, have mercy.
P. **Christ, have mercy.**
C. Lord, have mercy.
P. **Lord, have mercy.**

THE GLORIA

If it is to be said, the Gloria *now follows. For the text, see inside the front cover.*

The priest collects the prayerful thoughts of everyone present.
C. Let us pray.
At the end of the Opening Prayer:
P. **Amen.**

LITURGY OF THE WORD

The reader goes to the lectern for the first reading. All sit and listen. To indicate the end, the reader adds:

All respond:
This is the word of the Lord.   C' Thanks be to God.

The cantor sings or recites the psalm, and the people respond.
When there is a second reading, it is read at the lectern as before. To indicate the end, the reader adds: This is the Word of the Lord. *All respond:* Thanks be to God.
Then the deacon (or the celebrant) goes to the lectern. He may be accompanied by ministers with incense and candles.

He sings: *The people answer:*

The Lord be with you.   C' And al-so with you.

The deacon (or celebrant) sings or says:

A reading from the holy gospel accord-ing to N.

He makes the sign of the cross on the book, and then on his forehead, lips, and breast. The people respond:

C Glo-ry to you, Lord.

Then, if incense is used, the deacon (or celebrant) incenses the book and proclaims the gospel.
At the end of the gospel, the deacon (or celebrant) adds:

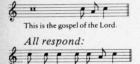

This is the gospel of the Lord.

All respond:

C Praise to you, Lord Je-sus Christ.

THE PROFESSION OF FAITH

If it is to be said, the Creed *now follows. For the text, see inside the front cover. The text of* The Apostles' Creed *is inside the back cover.*
The Prayer of the Faithful *now follows.*

THE LITURGY OF THE EUCHARIST

A song, chant, anthem or other suitable hymn may be sung as the gifts are brought to the altar. If there is no antiphon or hymn, the celebrant may say the following prayers in an audible voice.

C. Blessed are you, Lord, God of all creation. Through your goodness we have this bread to offer, which earth has given and human hands have made. It will become for us the bread of life.

P. **Blessed be God for ever.** (*Omitted if singing is in progress.*)

C. Blessed are you, Lord, God of all creation. Through your goodness we have this wine to offer, fruit of the vine and work of human hands. It will become our spiritual drink.

P. **Blessed be God for ever.** (*Omitted if singing is in progress.*)

After washing his hands the celebrant says:
Pray, brethren, that our sacrifice may be acceptable to God, the almighty Father.

P. **May the Lord accept the sacrifice at your hands**
for the praise and glory of his name,
for our good, and the good of all his Church.

The celebrant then reads the Prayer over the Gifts, *at the end of which:*
P. **Amen.**

THE EUCHARISTIC PRAYER

The celebrant begins the Eucharistic Prayer. *With hands extended, he sings:*

P The Lord be with you.   C And al-so with you.

P Lift up your hearts.   C We lift them up to the Lord.

P Let us give thanks to the Lord our God.

C It is right to give him thanks and praise.

At the end of the Preface, *the* Sanctus *is sung or said.*

The Eucharistic Prayer *of praise and thanksgiving is the centre and high point of the whole celebration. The congregation joins Christ in acknowledging the works of God and in offering his sacrifice to the Father.*

After the consecration, the celebrant sings:

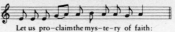

Let us pro-claim the mys-te-ry of faith:

The people reply using one of these acclamations:

1. **Christ has died,**
Christ is risen,
Christ will come again.

2. **Dying you destroyed our death,**
rising you restored our life.
Lord Jesus, come in glory.

3. **When we eat this bread and drink this cup,**
we proclaim your death, Lord Jesus,
until you come in glory.

4. **Lord, by your cross and resurrection**
you have set us free.
You are the Saviour of the world.

At the end of the Eucharistic Prayer, *the celebrant sings:*

Through him, with him, in him, in the u-ni-ty of the

Ho-ly Spir-it, all glo-ry and hon-our is yours, al-

The people respond:

might-y Fa-ther, for ev-er and ev-er.   C A-men.

THE COMMUNION RITE

The celebrant introduces the Lord's Prayer *in these or similar words.*

C. Let us pray with confidence to the Father in the words our Saviour gave us:

P. **Our Father, who art in heaven,**
hallowed be thy name.
Thy kingdom come.
Thy will be done on earth, as it is in heaven.

Give us this day our daily bread,
and forgive us our trespasses,
as we forgive those who trespass against us,
and lead us not into temptation,
but deliver us from evil.

C. Deliver us, Lord, from every evil,
and grant us peace in our day.
In your mercy keep us free from sin
and protect us from all anxiety
as we wait in joyful hope
for the coming of our Saviour, Jesus Christ.

P. For the kingdom, the power, and the glory
are yours, now and for ever.

C. Lord Jesus Christ, you said to your apostles:
I leave you peace, my peace I give you.
Look not on our sins, but on the faith of
your Church, and grant us the peace and
unity of your kingdom where you live for
ever and ever.

P. Amen.

C. The peace of the Lord be with you always.

P. And also with you.

C. Let us offer each other the sign of peace.

Lamb of God, you take away the sins of the
world : have mercy on us.
Lamb of God, you take away the sins of the
world : have mercy on us.
Lamb of God, you take away the sins of the
world : grant us peace.

*The celebrant genuflects and raising the host
says:*
This is the Lamb of God
who takes away the sins of the world.
Happy are those who are called to his supper.

Lord, I am not worthy to receive you,
but only say the word and I shall be healed.

*Communion over, the celebrant may sit for a
time, while all continue to make their*

*thanksgiving. Then, standing, the celebrant
says:*

Let us pray.

At the end of the prayer:

P. Amen.

THE CONCLUDING RITE

or:

ORD AN AIFRINN

Sagart: In ainm an Athar agus an Mhic agus an Spioraid Naoimh.
Pobal: **Amen.**

S. Go raibh an Tiarna libh.

Nó:

S. Grásta ár dTiarna Íosa Chríost agus grá Dé agus cumann an Spioraid Naoimh libh go léir.
P. **Agus leat féin.**

GNÍOMH AITHRÍ

S. A bhráithre tugaimis ár bpeacaí chun cuimhne chun go mb'fhiú sinn an tAifreann a cheiliúradh.

S. & P. **Admhaím do Dhia uilechumhachtach agus daoibhse, a bhráithre, gur pheacaigh mé go trom le smaoineamh agus le briathar, le gníomh agus le faillí, trí mo choir féin, trí mo choir féin, trí mo mhórchoir féin. Ar an ábhar sin, impím ar Naomh Mhuire síorÓgh, ar na haingil agus ar na naoimh, agus oraibhse, a bhráithre, guí ar mo shon chun an Tiarna Dia.**

S. Go ndéana Dia uilechumhachtach trócaire orainn, go maithe sé ár bpeacaí dúinn, agus go dtreoraí sé chun na beatha síoraí sinn.
P. **Amen.**
P. A Thiarna, déan trócaire.
P. **A Thiarna, déan trócaire.**
S. A Chríost, déan trócaire.
P. **A Chríost, déan trócaire.**
S. A Thiarna, déan trócaire.
P. **A Thiarna, déan trócaire.**

Nó:

S. A Thiarna, déan trócaire, ós tú a cuireadh chugainn chun lucht an chroíbhrú a leigheas.
P. **A Thiarna, déan trócaire.**
S. A Chríost, déan trócaire, ós tú a tháinig chun na peacaigh a thabhairt chun aithrí.
P. **A Chríost, déan trócaire.**
S. A Thiarna, déan trócaire, ós tú atá i do shuí ar dheasláimh an Athar chun idirghuí a dhéanamh ar ár son.
P. **A Thiarna, déan trócaire.**
S. Go ndéana Dia uilechumhachtach trócaire orainn, go maithe sé ár bpeacaí dúinn, agus go dtreoraí sé chun na beatha síoraí sinn.
P. **Amen.**

AN GHLÓIR

S. Glóir do Dhia sna harda,
S. & P. **Agus ar talamh síocháin do lucht a pháirte. Molaimid thú. Móraimid thú. Adhraimid thú. Tugaimid glóir duit. Gabhaimid buíochas leat as ucht do mhórghlóire. A Thiarna Dia, a Rí na bhflaitheas, A Dhia, a Athair uilechumhachtaigh, A Thiarna, a Aon-Mhic, a Íosa Chríost. A Thiarna Dia, a Uain Dé, Mac an Athar. Tusa, a thógann peacaí an domhain, déan trócaire orainn. Tusa a thógann peacaí an domhain, glac lenár nguí. Tusa atá i do shuí ar dheis an Athar, déan trócaire orainn. Óir is tú amháin is naofa. Is tú amháin is Tiarna. Is tú amháin is ró-ard, a Íosa Críost, mar aon leis an Spiorad Naomh i nglóir Dé an tAthair. Amen.**

AN URNAÍ

S. Guímis: . . .   P. **Amen.**

LIOTÚIRGE AN BHRIATHAIR

Léitear an chéad léacht agus ag an deireadh:
L. Sin é Briathar Dé.
P. **Buíochas le Dia.**

Cantar an Salm agus ansin léitear an dara léacht.
L. Sin é Briathar Dé.
P. **Buíochas le Dia.**

Seasann an pobal. Cantar an Alleluia.
S. Go raibh an Tiarna libh.
P. **Agus leat féin.**
S. Sliocht as an Soiscéal naofa de réir N.A.
P. **Glóir duit, a Thiarna.**
S. Sin é Soiscéal Dé.
P. **Moladh duit, a Chríost.**

AN CHRÉ

Éiríonn an pobal ina seasamh.

S. Creidim in aon Dia amháin.
S. & P. **An tAthair uilechumhachtach a rinne neamh agus talamh agus an uile ní sofheicthe agus dofheicthe. agus in aon Tiarna amháin, Íosa Críost, Aon-Mhic Dé, an té a rugadh ón Athair sula raibh aon saol ann, Dia ó Dhia, solas ó sholas fíorDhia ó fhíorDhia; an té a gineadh agus nach ndearnadh, agus atá d'aon substaint leis an Athair; is tríd a rinneadh an uile ní. Ar ár son-na an cine daonna, agus ar son ár slánaithe, thuirling sé ó neamh.**

Cromtar an ceann.

Ionchollaíodh le cumhacht an Spioraid Naoimh é i mbroinn na Maighdine Muire agus ghlac sé nádúr daonna. Céasadh ar an gcrois é freisin ar ár son; d'fhulaing sé páis faoi Phontius Pioláit agus adhlacadh é.

10

D'aiséirigh an treas lá
de réir na scrioptúr;
chuaigh suas ar neamh;
tá ina shuí ar dheis an Athar.
Tiocfaidh sé an athuair faoi ghlóir
le breithiúnas a thabhairt
ar bheo agus ar mhairbh,
agus ní bheidh deireadh lena ríocht.
Creidim sa Spiorad Naomh,
Tiarna agus bronntóir na beatha,
an té a ghluaiseann ón Athair agus ón Mac.
Tugtar dó adhradh agus glóir
mar aon leis an Athair agus leis an Mac:
is é a labhair trí na fáithe.
Creidim san aon Eaglais
naofa, chaitliceach, aspalda.
Admhaím an t-aon bhaisteadh amháin
chun maithiúnas na bpeacaí.
Agus táim ag súil le haiséirí na marbh
agus le beatha an tsaoil atá le teacht.
Amen.

Leantar le Guí an Phobail.

LIOTÚIRGE NA hEOCAIRISTE

*Suíonn an pobal. Le linn na n-ofrálacha a
bheith á n-iompar agus á dtoirbhirt is ionmholta
iomann a chanadh.*

*Mura gcantar iomann ofrála, deir ag sagart
os ard:*

S. Is beannaithe thú a Thiarna, a Dhia na
cruinne mar gur bhronn tú orainn an t-arán
seo a ofrálaimid duit.
An talamh agus saothar an duine
a thugann é mar thoradh
agus déanfar de arán na beatha dúinn.
P. **Moladh go deo le Dia.**

S. Is beannaithe thú a Thiarna, a Dhia na cruinne
mar gur bhronn tú orainn an fíon seo
a ofrálaimid duit.
An fhíniúin agus saothar an duine
a thugann é mar thoradh
agus déanfar de deoch spioradálta dúinn.
P. **Moladh go deo le Dia.**

S. Guígí, a bhráithre, go nglaca Dia an tAthair
uilechumhachtach leis an íobairt seo uaimse
agus uaibhse.

P. **Go nglaca an Tiarna
leis an íobairt seo ó do lámha
chun onóra agus glóire a ainm,
agus chun sochair dúinne
agus dá NaomhEaglais uile.**

*Léann an sagart an Urnaí os cionn na
nOfrálacha.*
P. **Amen.**

AN PHAIDIR EOCAIRISTEACH

Léitear an Phreafáid

S.&P. **Is naofa, naofa, naofa thú,
a Thiarna, Dia na slua.
Tá neamh agus talamh lán de do ghlóir.
Hósanna sna harda.
Is beannaithe an té atá ag teacht in ainm an
Tiarna.
Hósanna sna harda.**

S. Fógraímis rúndiamhair an chreidimh.

Freagraíonn an pobal de chomhgháir:
**A Íosa, fuair tú bás ar ár son.
D'éirigh tú ó na mairbh.
Tiocfaidh tú arís.**
Nó:
**Táimid ag fógairt do bháis, a Thiarna Íosa,
agus ag comóradh d'aiséirí, nó go dtaga tú.**
Nó:
**Gach uair a ithimid an t-arán seo
agus a ólaimid an chailís seo,
fógraimid do bhás, a Thiarna Íosa,
nó go dtaga tú.**
Nó:
**Is iad do bhás agus d'aiséirí a shaor sinn, a
Thiarna.
Is tú Slánaitheoir an domhain.**
Nó:
Mo Thiarna agus mo Dhia.

S. Is tríd, agus leis, agus ann a thugtar gach
onóir agus glóir duitse,
a Dhia, an tAthair uilechumhachtach, mar
aon leis an Spiorad Naomh,
trí shaol na saol.
P. **Amen.**

DEASGHNÁTHA NA COMAOINEACH

S. Guímis chun an Athar faoi mar a mhúin ár
Slánaitheoir dúinn a dhéanamh:
S.&P. **Ár nAthair atá ar neamh,
go naofar d'ainm,
go dtaga do ríocht,
go ndéantar do thoil ar an talamh, mar a
dhéantar ar neamh.
Ár n-arán laethúil tabhair dúinn inniu,
Agus maith dúinn ár bhfiacha, mar a
mhaithimidne dár bhféichiúna féin,
agus ná lig sinn i gcathú,
ach saor sinn ó olc.**

11

S. Saor sinn ó gach olc, impímid ort, a Thiarna.
Tabhair dúinn síocháin lenár linn, ionas go
mbeimid, le cabhair do thrócaire,
saor ón bpeaca i gcónaí agus slán ón uile
bhuairt
agus sinn ag súil go lúcháireach le teacht ár
Slánaitheora, Íosa Críost.

P. Óir is leatsa an ríocht agus an chumhacht
agus an ghlóir trí shaol na saol.

S. A Thiarna Íosa Críost, a dúirt le d'Aspail:
Fágaim síocháin agaibh,
tugaim daoibh mo shíocháin: ná féach ar ár
bpeacaíne ach ar chreideamh d'Eaglaise.
Tabhair síocháin di agus aontaigh í ina
chéile, faoi mar is toil leat féin.
tusa a mhaireann agus a rialaíonn trí shaol
na saol.

P. **Amen.**

S. Síocháin an Tiarna libh i gcónaí.

P. **Agus leat féin.**

S. Cuirigí in iúl dá chéile go bhfuil síocháin
eadraibh.
**A Uain Dé, a thógann peacaí an domhain,
déan trócaire orainn.**
**A Uain Dé, a thógann peacaí an domhain,
déan trócaire orainn.**
**A Uain Dé, a thógann peacaí an domhain,
tabhair dúinn síocháin.**

S. Seo é Uan Dé, seo é an té a thógann peacaí
an domhain. Is méanar dóibh siúd a fuair
cuireadh chun séire an Uain.

*Ansin deir sé aon uair amháin i gcomhar leis an
bpobal:*

S.&P. **A Thiarna, ní fiú mé go dtiocfá faoi mo
dhíon, ach abairse an focal agus leigheasfar
m'anam.**

IARGOMAOINEACH

Ag deireadh na hurnaí:

P. **Amen.**

AN DÚNADH

S. Go raibh an Tiarna libh.

P. **Agus leat féin.**

S. Go mbeannaí Dia uilechumhachtach sibh,
Athair, Mac agus Spiorad Naomh.

P. **Amen.**

S. Tá an tAifreann thart. Imígí faoi shíocháin.
Nó:
Go dté sibh slán faoi shíocháin Chríost.
Nó:
Imígí faoi shíocháin chun grá agus
seirbhís a thabhairt don Tiarna.

P. **Buíochas le Dia.**

ORDO MISSAE

THE INTRODUCTORY RITES

The Mass may begin with the singing or recitation of the Entrance Antiphon *or a* Hymn *whilst the celebrant and servers approach the altar. The people stand.*

Celebrant: In nomine Patris, et Filii, et Spiritus Sancti.
People: **Amen.**

One of the following greetings is used:
1.
C. Gratia Domini nostri Iesu Christi, et caritas Dei, et communicatio Sancti Spiritus sit cum omnibus vobis.
P. **Et cum spiritu tuo.**
2.
C. Gratia vobis et pax a Deo Patre nostro et Domino Iesu Christo.
P. **Benedictus Deus et Pater Domini nostri Iesu Christi.**
Or **Et cum spiritu tuo.**
3.
C. Dominus vobiscum.
P. **Et cum spiritu tuo.**

THE PENITENTIAL RITE

The celebrant invites the people to repent of their sins using one of the following forms:
1.
C. Fratres, agnoscamus peccata nostra, ut apti simus ad sacra mysteria celebranda.
After a brief silence all say:
Confiteor Deo omnipotenti et vobis, fratres, quia peccavi nimis cogitatione, verbo, opere et omissione:
(*all strike their breast*)
mea culpa, mea culpa, mea maxima culpa. Ideo precor beatam Mariam semper Virginem; omnes Angelos et Sanctos, et vos, fratres, orare pro me ad Dominum Deum nostrum.

2.
C. Fratres, agnoscamus peccata nostra, ut apti simus ad sacra mysteria celebranda.
After a brief silence the celebrant continues:
Miserere nostri, Domine.
P. **Quia peccavimus tibi.**
C. Ostende nobis, Domine, misericordiam tuam.
P. **Et salutare tuum da nobis.**
3.
C. Fratres, agnoscamus peccata nostra, ut apti simus ad sacra mysteria celebranda.

After a brief silence the celebrant says the following, or similar words. The people's response, however, remains the same.

Qui missus es sanare contritos corde : Kyrie, eleison.
P. **Kyrie, eleison.**
C. Qui peccatores vocare venisti : Christe, eleison.
P. **Christe, eleison.**
C. Qui ad dexteram Patris sedes, ad interpellandum pro nobis : Kyrie eleison.
P. **Kyrie, eleison.**

The Act of Penance *is followed by the* Absolution.
C. Misereatur nostri omnipotens Deus et, dimissis peccatis nostris, perducat nos ad vitam aeternam.
P. **Amen.**

Ký-ri- e, e-lé- i-son. ij. Christe, e-lé-

i-son. ij. Ký-ri- e, e-lé- i-son. Ký-ri- e, e-

lé- i-son.

THE GLORIA

If it is to be said, the Gloria *now follows:*

Gloria in excelsis Deo et in terra pax hominibus bonae voluntatis. Laudamus te, benedicimus te, adoramus te, glorificamus te, gratias agimus tibi propter magnam gloriam tuam, Domine Deus, Rex caelestis, Deus Pater omnipotens. Domine Fili unigenite, Iesu Christe, Domine Deus, Agnus Dei, Filius Patris, qui tollis peccata mundi, miserere nobis; qui tollis peccata mundi, suscipe deprecationem nostram. Qui sedes ad dexteram Patris, miserere nobis. Quoniam tu solus Sanctus, tu solus Dominus, tu solus Altissimus, Iesu Christe, cum Sancto Spiritu : in gloria Dei Patris. Amen.

The priest collects the prayerful thoughts of everyone present.
C. Oremus.
At the end of the Opening Prayer:
P. **Amen.**

LITURGY OF THE WORD

After the first reading:

Verbum Dómi-ni. ℟. De- o grá-ti- as.

After the second reading:

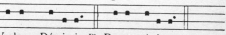

Verbum Dómi-ni. ℟. De- o grá-ti- as.

Before the Gospel:

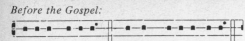

Dómi-nus vobíscum. ℟. Et cum spíri-tu tu-o.

Lécti-o sancti Evangé-li-i secúndum N...

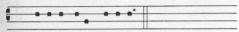

℟. Gló-ri-a tibi, Dómine.

After the Gospel:

Verbum Dómini. ℟. Laus tibi, Christe.

THE PROFESSION OF FAITH

If it is to be said, the Creed *now follows:*
Credo in unum Deum,
Patrem omnipotentem, factorem caeli et terrae,
visibilium omnium et invisibilium.

Et in unum Dominum Iesum Christum,
Filium Dei unigenitum,
et ex Patre natum ante omnia saecula.
Deum de Deo, lumen de lumine, Deum verum
de Deo vero,
genitum, non factum, consubstantialem Patri:
per quem omnia facta sunt.
Qui propter nos homines et propter nostram
salutem descendit de caelis.
Et incarnatus est de Spiritu Sancto
ex Maria Virgine, et homo factus est.
Crucifixus etiam pro nobis sub Pontio Pilato;
passus et sepultus est,
et resurrexit tertia die, secundum Scripturas,
et ascendit in caelum, sedet ad dexteram Patris.
Et iterum venturus est cum gloria, iudicare
vivos et mortuos,
cuius regni non erit finis.
Et in Spiritum Sanctum, Dominum et
vivificantem,

qui ex Patre Filioque procedit.
Qui cum Patre et Filio simul adoratur et
conglorificatur:
qui locutus est per prophetas.
Et unam, sanctam, catholicam et apostolicam
Ecclesiam.
Confiteor unum baptisma in remissionem
peccatorum.
Et exspecto resurrectionem mortuorum,
et vitam venturi saeculi. Amen.

The Prayer of the Faithful *now follows.*

THE LITURGY OF THE EUCHARIST

*A song, chant, anthem or other suitable hymn
may be sung as the gifts are brought to the
altar. If there is no antiphon or hymn, the
celebrant may say the following prayers in an
audible voice.*
C. Benedictus es, Domine, Deus universi,
quia de tua largitate accepimus panem,
quem tibi offerimus,
fructum terrae et operis manuum hominum,
ex quo nobis fiet panis vitae.
P. **Benedictus Deus in saecula.** (*Omitted if
singing is in progress.*)
C. Benedictus es, Domine, Deus universi,
quia de tua largitate accepimus vinum,
quod tibi offerimus,
fructum vitis et operis manuum hominum,
ex quo nobis fiet potus spiritalis.
P. **Benedictus Deus in saecula.** (*Omitted if
singing is in progress.*)
After washing his hands the celebrant says:
Orate, fratres:
ut meum ac vestrum sacrificium
acceptabile fiat apud Deum Patrem
omnipotentem.
P. **Suscipiat Dominus sacrificium de manibus
tuis
ad laudem et gloriam nominis sui,
ad utilitatem quoque nostram
totiusque Ecclesiae suae sanctae.**

The celebrant then reads the Prayer over the
Gifts, *at the end of which:*
P. **Amen.**

THE EUCHARISTIC PRAYER

Before the Preface:

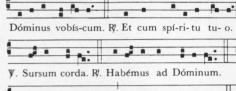

Dóminus vobís-cum. ℟. Et cum spí-ri-tu tu-o.

℣. Sursum corda. ℟. Habémus ad Dóminum.

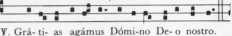

℣. Grá-ti-as agámus Dómi-no De-o nostro.

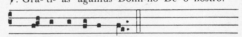

℟. Dignum et iustum est.

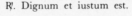

S anctus, * Sanctus, Sanctus Dóminus De-us Sába-oth. Pleni sunt cæ-li et terra gló-ri-a tu-a. Hosánna in excélsis. Benedíctus qui ve-nit in nómi-ne Dómini. Ho-sánna in excélsis.

Acclamation after the Consecration:

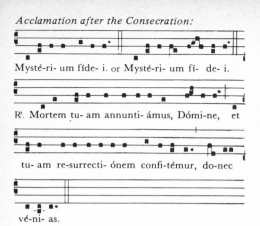

Mysté-ri- um fíde- i. or Mysté-ri-um fí- de- i.

℞. Mortem tu- am annunti- ámus, Dómi-ne, et

tu- am re-surrecti- ónem confi-témur, do-nec

vé-ni- as.

2.
Quotiescumque manducamus panem hunc
et calicem bibimus,
mortem tuam annuntiamus, Domine, donec
venias.

3.
Salvator mundi, salva nos,
qui per crucem et resurrectionem tuam
liberasti nos.

After the Doxology:

... per ómni- a sǽcu-la sæcu-ló- rum. ℞. Amen.

THE COMMUNION RITE

The celebrant introduces the Lord's Prayer *in these or similar words.*

C. Præceptis salutaribus moniti,
et divina institutione formati,
audemus dicere:

P. Pater noster, qui es in cælis:
sanctificetur nomen tuum;
adveniat regnum tuum;
fiat voluntas tua, sicut in cælo, et in terra.
Panem nostrum cotidianum da nobis hodie;
et dimitte nobis debita nostra,
sicut et nos dimittimus debitoribus nostris;
et ne nos inducas in tentationem;
sed libera nos a malo.

C. Libera nos, quæsumus, Domine, ab omnibus
malis,
da propitius pacem in diebus nostris,
ut, ope misericordiæ tuæ adiuti,
et a peccato simus semper liberi
et ab omni perturbatione securi:
exspectantes beatam spem
et adventum Salvatoris nostri Iesu Christi.

P. Quia tuum est regnum,
et potestas, et gloria
in sæcula.

C. Domine Iesu Christe, qui dixisti Apostolis tuis:
Pacem relinquo vobis, pacem meam do vobis:
ne respicias peccata nostra,
sed fidem Ecclesiæ tuæ;
eamque secundum voluntatem tuam
pacificare et coadunare digneris.
Qui vivis et regnas in sæcula sæculorum.

P. Amen.

C. Pax Domini sit semper vobiscum.

P. Et cum spiritu tuo.

C. Offerte vobis pacem.

Agnus Dei, qui tollis peccata mundi:
miserere nobis.
Agnus Dei, qui tollis peccata mundi:
miserere nobis.
Agnus Dei, qui tollis peccata mundi: dona
nobis pacem.

The celebrant genuflects, and raising the host says:
Ecce Agnus Dei, ecce qui tollit peccata
mundi.
Beati qui ad cenam Agni vocati sunt.

Domine, non sum dignus, ut intres sub
tectum meum:
sed tantum dic verbo, et sanabitur anima mea.

Communion over, the celebrant may sit for a time, while all continue to make their thanksgiving. Then, standing, the celebrant says:

Oremus.

At the end of the prayer:

P. Amen.

THE CONCLUDING RITE

C. Dominus vobiscum.

P. Et cum spiritu tuo.

C. Benedicat vos omnipotens Deus,
Pater, et Filius, et Spiritus Sanctus.

P. Amen.

The Dismissal:

I-te, mis- sa est.

℞. De- o grá- ti- as.

On Easter Sunday, during the Easter Octave and on Whit Sunday:

I-te, missa est, alle-lú-ia, alle- lú- ia.
℞. De- o grá-ti- as, alle-lú-ia, alle- lú- ia.

1. Abide with me
H.F. Lyte (1793-1847)

Abide with me, fast falls the eventide;
the darkness deepens, Lord, with me abide!
When other helpers fail, and comforts flee,
help of the helpless, O abide with me.
2
Swift to its close ebbs out life's little day;
earth's joys grow dim, its glories pass away;
change and decay in all around I see;
O thou who changest not, abide with me.
3
I need thy presence every passing hour;
what but thy grace can foil the
tempter's power?
Who like thyself my guide and stay can be?
Through cloud and sunshine, O abide
with me.
4
I fear no foe with thee at hand to bless;
ills have no weight, and tears no bitterness.
Where is death's sting? Where, grave,
thy victory?
I triumph still, if thou abide with me.
5
Hold thou thy cross before my closing eyes;
shine through the gloom, and point me
to the skies;
heaven's morning breaks, and earth's vain
shadows flee:
in life, in death, O Lord, abide with me!

2. Ag Críost an Síol
Traidisiúnta

Ag Críost an síol, ag Críost an fómhar,
in iothlainn Dé go dtugtar sinn.

Ag Críost an mhuir, ag Críost an t-iasc,
i líonta Dé go gcastar sinn.

Ó fhás go haois, is ó aois go bás.
Do dhá láimh, a Chríost, anall tharainn.

Ó bhás go críoch, ní críoch ach athfhás,
i bParthas na nGrást go rabhaimid.

3. Adeste Fideles

Adeste fideles.
laeti triumphantes;
venite, venite in Bethlehem;
natum videte
regem angelorum:
Venite adoremus, (2)
venite adoremus Dominium.
2
Deum de Deo,
lumen de lumine,
gestant puellae viscera:
Deum verum,
genitum, non factum:
3
Cantet nunc Io!
Chorus angelorum;
cantet nunc aula caelestium:
Gloria
in excelsis Deo!
4
Ergo qui natus
die hodierna,
Jesu tibi sit gloria:
Patris aeterni
Verbum caro factum!

4. All Creatures of our God and King
W. H. Draper (1855-1933)
Based on the Cantico di Frate Sole of
St Francis of Assisi (1182-1226)

All creatures of our God and King,
lift up your voice and with us sing
alleluia, alleluia!
Thou burning sun with golden beam,
thou silver moon with softer gleam:
O praise him. O praise him,
alleluia, alleluia, alleluia.
2
Thou rushing wind that art so strong,
ye clouds that sail in heaven along,
O praise him, alleluia!
Thou rising morn, in praise rejoice,
ye lights of evening, find a voice:
3
Thou flowing water, pure and clear,
make music for thy Lord to hear,
alleluia, alleluia!
Thou fire so masterful and bright,
that givest man both warmth and light:
4
Dear mother earth, who day by day
unfoldest blessings on our way,
O praise him, alleluia!
The flowers and fruits that in thee grow
let them his glory also show:
5
And all ye men of tender heart,
forgiving others, take your part,
O sing ye, alleluia!
Ye who long pain and sorrow bear,
praise God and on him cast your care:
6
And thou, most kind and gentle death,
waiting to hush our latest breath,
O praise him, alleluia!
Thou leadest home the child of God,
and Christ our Lord the way hath trod:
7
Let all things their creator bless,
and worship him in humbleness,
O praise him, alleluia!
Praise, praise the Father, praise the Son,
and praise the Spirit, Three in One:

Alleluia, for your Gospel, O Lord.

5

Alleluia, alleluia, alleluia!

For your Gospel, O Lord Jesus
is good news for your people.
2
For your Gospel, O Lord Jesus,
fills our souls with its gladness.
3
For your Gospel, O Lord Jesus,
lights the torch of true wisdom.
4
For your Gospel, O Lord Jesus,
is a fire which consumes us.
5
For your Gospel, O Lord Jesus,
judges man through all ages.

Alleluia Psalm 150

6

Jan Vermulst/Omer Westendorf

Alleluia, alleluia, alleluia.
Praise God in his holy dwelling;
praise him on his mighty throne;
praise him for his wonderful deeds;
praise him for his sov'reign majesty.
2
Praise him with the blast of trumpet;
praise him now with lyre and harps;
praise him with the timbrel and dance;
praise him with the sound of string and reed.
3
Praise him with resounding cymbals;
with cymbals that crash, give praise;
O let ev'rything that has breath,
let all living creatures praise the Lord.
4
Praise God, the almighty Father;
praise Christ, his beloved Son;
give praise to the Spirit of love.
For ever the triune God be praised.

All Glory, Praise and Honour

7

Sr Theodulph of Orleans (760-821)
tr. J. M. Neale

All glory, praise and honour,
to you, redeemer King,
for whom the children's voices
made glad Hosannas ring.
You are the King of Israel,
and David's royal Son,
who in the Lord's name comes to us,
the King and blessed one.
2
The company of angels
are praising you on high;
and mortal men and all things
created make reply.
The people of the Hebrews
with palms before you went;
our praise and prayer and anthems
before you we present.
3
To you, before your passion,
they sang their hymns of praise;
to you, now high exalted,
our melody we raise.
As once you did accept their praise,
accept this praise we sing,
you who rejoice in every good,
our good and gracious King.

All people that on earth do dwell

8

All people that on earth do dwell
Sing to the Lord with cheerful voice
Him serve with fear, his praise forth tell,
Come ye before him and rejoice.
2
The Lord ye know is God indeed.
Without our aid he did us make.
We are his folk, he doth us feed,
And for his sheep he doth us take.

3
O enter then his gates with praise.
Approach with joy his courts unto.
Praise laud and bless his name always
For it is seemly so to do.
4
For why? The Lord our God is good:
His mercy is forever sure.
His truth at all times firmly stood,
And shall from age to age endure.
5
To Father, Son and Holy Ghost,
The God whom heaven and earth adore,
From men and from the angel host
Be praise and glory evermore.
Amen.

All the earth proclaim the Lord

9

Lucien Deiss (based on Psalm 100)

All the earth proclaim the Lord,
sing your praise to God.
Serve you the Lord, heart filled with
gladness.
Come into his presence, singing for joy.
2
Know that the Lord is our creator.
Yes, he is our Father, we are his sons.
3
We are the sheep of his green pasture,
for we are his people, he is our God.
4
Enter his gates bringing thanksgiving,
O enter his courts while singing his praise.
5
Our Lord is good, his love enduring,
his Word is abiding now with all men.
6
Honour and praise be to the Father,
the Son, and the Spirit, world without end.

All you Nations
10
Psalm 65 (Lucien Deiss)

All you nations,
sing out your joy to the Lord,
alleluia, alleluia.

Joyfully shout, all you on earth,
give praise to the glory of God;
and with a hymn, sing out
his glorious praise:
alleluia.
2
Let all the earth kneel in his sight,
extolling his marvellous fame;
honour his name, in highest heaven
give praise:
alleluia.
3
Come forth and see all the great works
that God has brought forth by his might;
fall on your knees before his
glorious throne:
alleluia.
4
Parting the seas with might and power,
he rescued his people from shame;
let us give thanks for all his
merciful deeds:
alleluia.
5.
Glory and thanks be to the Father;
honour and praise to the Son;
and to the Spirit, source of life
and of love:
alleluia.

Almighty Father, Lord Most High
11

Almighty Father, Lord most high
Who madest all, who fillest all,
Thy name we praise and magnify,
For all our needs on thee we call.

2
We offer to thee of thine own
Ourselves and all that we can bring,
In bread and cup before thee shown,
Our universal offering.
3
All that we have we bring to thee.
Yet all is naught when all is done.
Save that in it thy love can see
The sacrifice of thy dear Son.
4
By his command in bread and cup
His body and his blood we plead:
What on the cross he offer'd up
Is here our sacrifice indeed.
5
For all thy gifts of life and grace,
Here we thy servants humbly pray.
That thou would'st look upon the face
Of thine anointed Son today.

A Íosa Bháin
12
Traidisiúnta

A Íosa bháin, id' láthair gheod,
ag caoi do bháis san ardchrois mhór,
Ó aois go bás ag tál na ndeor,
'Sag maíomh mo ghrá don Slánaitheoir.
Ó a Shlánaitheoir, Ó a Shlánaitheoir.
2
Mo dhíon, mo ghrá, mo scáth, mo threoir,
An íobairt ard, ofráil mo stóir,
an fhíonfhuil naofa buan 'san fheoil:
sin maoin im láimh óm Shlánaitheoir.
Ó a Shlánaitheoir, Ó a Shlánaitheoir.

An tAiséirí
13

'S é Íosa an fíréan a shaothraigh ár n-anam,
'Sé rinnemuid a cheannacht ón ndaoirse;
Is d'fhulaing sé páis agus bás ar an gcroich,
Mar gheall ar na peacaí a dhéan 'mid.
Agus aililiú lá, aililiú ló.
Ailililiú ó.
Má mhaslaítear an cholainn,
Ní baolach don anam,
Ach ná séanaigí m'ainmse choíche.

Angels we have heard on high
14
James Chadwick (1813-82)

Angels we have heard on high,
sweetly singing o'er the plains,
and the mountains in reply
echo still their joyous strains.
Gloria in excelsis Deo. (2)
2
Shepherds, why this jubilee?
Why your rapturous strain prolong?
Say, what may your tidings be,
which inspire your heavenly song.
3
Come to Bethlehem and see
him whose birth the angels sing;
come, adore on bended knee
the infant Christ, the new-born King.
4
See within a manger laid,
Jesus, Lord of heaven and earth!
Mary, Joseph, lend your aid
to celebrate our Saviour's birth.

A Rí an Domhnaigh

15

Tomás Rua Ó Súilleabháin

A Rí an Domhnaigh, tar le cabhair chugam
is fóir in am ón bpian mé.
A Rí an Luain ghil, bíse buan liom
is ná lig uaitse féin mé.
A Rí na Márta, a chroí na páirte,
déan díonadh Lá an tSléibh' dom.
A Rí Céadaoine, saor ó ghéibheann mé,
cé fad' óm chaoimhghein féin mé.

2

A Rí Déardaoine, maith ár bpeacaíne
a rinne do dhlí a réabadh.
A Rí na hAoine, ná coinnigh cuimhne
ar mo dhroch-ghníomhartha baotha.
A Rí an tSathairn, go síoraí achainím
mé 'thabhairt thar Acheron caorthin',
faoi dhíon do thearmainn, trí ríocht an Aifrinn,
suas go Párthas naofa.

Attende Domine

16

*Attende Domine, et miserere,
quia preccavimus tibi.*

Ad te Rex summe, omnium redemptor,
oculos nostros sublevamus flentes:
exaudi, Christe, supplicantum preces.

2

Dextera Patris, lapis angularis,
via salutis, janua caelestis,
ablue nostri maculas delicti.

3

Rogamus, Deus, tuam majestatem̦:
auribus sacris gemitus exaudi:
crimina nostra placidus indulge.

4

Tibi fatemur crimina admissa:
contrito corde pandimus occulta:
tua, Redemptor, pietas ignoscat.

5

Innocens captus, nec repugnans dectus,
testibus falsis pro impiis damnatus:
quos redemisti, tu conserva, Christe.

At the Cross her Vigil Keeping

17

*Ascribed to Jacopone da
Todi (d. 1306).
Abridged translation by Anthony Petti.*

At the cross her vigil keeping,
Mary stood in sorrow, weeping,
when her Son was crucified.

2

While she waited in her anguish,
seeing Christ in torment languish,
bitter sorrow pierced her heart.

3

With what pain and desolation,
with what noble resignation,
Mary watched her dying Son.

4

Ever patient in her yearning,
though her tear-filled eyes were burning,
Mary gazed upon her Son.

5

Who, that sorrow contemplating,
on that passion meditating,
would not share the Virgin's grief?

6

Christ she saw, for our salvation,
scourged with cruel acclamation,
bruised and beaten by the rod.

7

Christ she saw with life-blood failing,
all her anguish unavailing,
saw him breathe his very last.

8

Mary, fount of love's devotion,
let me share with true emotion
all the sorrow you endured.

9

Virgin, ever interceding,
hear me in my fervent pleading:
fire me with your love of Christ.

10

Mother, may this prayer be granted:
that Christ's love may be implanted
in the depths of my poor soul.

11

At the cross, your sorrow sharing,
all your grief and torment bearing,
let me stand and mourn with you.

12

Fairest maid of all creation,
Queen of hope and consolation,
let me feel your grief sublime.

13

Virgin, in your love befriend me,
at the Judgement Day defend me,
help me by your constant prayer.

14

Saviour, when my life shall leave me,
through your mother's prayers receive me
with the fruits of victory.

15

Let me to your love be taken,
let my soul in death awaken
to the joys of Paradise.

Away in a manger
Author Unknown

18

Away in a manger,
no crib for a bed,
the little Lord Jesus
laid down his sweet head.
The stars in the bright sky
looked down where he lay,
the little Lord Jesus
asleep on the hay.
2
The cattle are lowing,
the baby awakes,
but little Lord Jesus
no crying he makes.
I love thee, Lord Jesus!
Look down from the sky,
and stay by my side
until morning is nigh.
3
Be near me, Lord Jesus:
I ask thee to stay
close by me for ever,
and love me, I pray.
Bless all the dear children
in thy tender care.
and fit us for heaven,
to live with thee there.

Behold a Virgin Bearing Him
M. Gannon

19

Behold a Virgin bearing him,
who comes to save us from our sin;
The prophets cry 'Prepare his way,
make straight his paths to Christmas Day.'
2
Behold our hope and life and light,
the promise of the holy night.
We lift our prayer and bend our knee
to his great love and majesty.

Be thou my Vision
*Irish (6th cent) tr. Mary Bryne,
versified by Eleanor Hull*

20

Be thou my vision, O Lord of my heart,
be all else but naught to me,
save that thou art;
be thou my best thought in the day
and the night,
both waking and sleeping, thy presence
my light.
2
Be thou my wisdom, be thou my true word,
be thou ever with me, and I with thee, Lord;
be thou my great Father, and I thy true son,
be thou in me dwelling, and I with thee one.
3
Riches I need not, nor man's empty praise,
be thou mine inheritance now and all days;
be thou and thou only the first in my heart,
the King of high heaven, my treasure
thou art.
4
High King of heaven, thou heaven's
bright sun.
O grant me its joys, after victory is won;
great heart of my own heart, whatever befall,
still be thou my vision. O ruler of all.

Bí 'Íosa im Chroíse
Traidisiunta

21

Bí 'Íosa im chroíse 's im chuimhne gach uair,
bí 'Íosa im chroíse le haithrí go luath,
bí 'Íosa im chroíse le dúthracht go buan,
's a Íosa, 'Dhia dhílis, ná scar choíche uaim.
2
'Sé Íosa mo ríse, mo chara 's mo ghrá.
'sé Íosa mo dhídean ar pheaca 's ar bhás.
'Sé Íosa mo aoibhneas, mo sheasamh de ghnáth,
's a Íosa, 'Dhia dhílis, ná scar liom go bráth.

3
Bí 'Íosa go síoraí im chroí is im bhéal,
bí 'Íosa go síoraí im thuiscint 's im mhéin,
bí 'Íosa go síoraí im mheabhair mar léann,
's, a Íosa, 'Dhia dhílis, ná fág mé liom féin.

Beannaigh sinn a Athair
Traidisiúnta

22

Beannaigh sinn a Athair,
agus beannaigh sinn a Chríost,
go gcumhdaí sibh ár n-anama go dtagaimid arís.
Beannacht leat a theach Dé, agus beannacht
Dé 'nár dtimpeall,
nár scara uainne grásta Dé go bhfillimid
chun a theampaill.

Blest are the pure in heart

23

Blest are the pure in heart,
Whose souls are filled with grace.
The joys of heaven shall be theirs:
To see God face to face.
2
Blest are the humble minds,
Which envy cannot snare,
Ambition has no pow'r to harm:
God's blessings they will share.
3
Blest are true men of peace,
Dispelling war and strife.
The peace of Christ is in their hearts,
They gain eternal life.
4
All those who suffer loss,
Enduring pain and grief,
The comfort of the Lord is theirs:
Christ brings them true relief.
5
Lord, keep us in your care,
Your mercy still impart.
And help us to preserve for you
A pure and perfect heart.

The Beatitudes
Aideen O'Sullivan,
based on Matt.5; Lk.23

24

Walk in love, giving thanks with joy to the Father.
He has called us to share his life.

Blessed are the poor in spirit,
the kingdom of heaven is theirs.
Blessed are those who mourn,
for they shall be comforted.
2
Blessed are the meek,
for they shall inherit the earth.
Blessed are those who hunger and thirst for
righteousness.
for they shall be satisfied.
3
Blessed are the merciful,
for they shall obtain mercy.
Blessed are the pure in heart,
for they shall see God.
4
Blessed are the peacemakers
for they shall be called sons of God.
Blessed are those who suffer for the cause of
right,
for theirs is the kingdom of heaven.

Alternative refrain:
Amen, truly I say to you,
this day you will be with me in paradise.

Bring all ye dear-bought nations
Wipo (11th cent)
tr. Walter Kirkham Blount

25

Bring, all ye dear-bought nations, bring,
alleluia,
your richest praises to your king,
alleluia,
that spotless Lamb, who more than due,
alleluia,

paid for his sheep, and those sheep you,
alleluia, alleluia, alleluia, alleluia.
2
Life died, but soon revived again,
and even death by it was slain,
Say, happy Magdalen, oh, say,
what didst thou see there by the way?
3
'I saw the tomb of my dear Lord,
I saw himself, and him adored,
I saw the napkin and the sheet,
that bound his head and wrapt his feet.'
4
'I heard the angels witness bear,
Jesus is ris'n; he is not there;
Go, tell his followers they shall see
thine and their hope in Galilee.'
5
We, Lord, with faithful hearts and voice,
on this thy rising day rejoice.
O thou, whose power o'ercame the grave,
by grace and love us sinners save.

Behold, O Lord, I come to do your will.
Psalm 39

26

Behold, O Lord, I come to do your will.

I waited, I waited for the Lord
and he stooped down to me;
he put a new song in my mouth,
praise of our God.
2
You do not ask for sacrifice and offerings,
but an open ear.
You do not ask for holocaust and victim.
Instead, here am I.
3
In the scroll of the book it stands written
that I should do your will.
My God, I delight in your law
in the depth of my heart.

4
Your justice I have proclaimed
in the great assembly.
My lips I have not sealed;
You know it, O Lord.
5
I have not hidden your justice in my heart,
but declared your faithful help.
I have not hidden your love and your truth
from the great assembly.
6
O let there be rejoicing and gladness
for all who seek you.
Let them say "The Lord is great",
who love your saving help.

Caomhnaigh mé a Thiarna
Caomhnaigh mé, a Thiarna,
is ortsa a thriallaim.

27

Is é an Tiarna is rogha liom;
mo chuid de réir oidhreachta,
agus cuid mo chailíse:
is ort atá mo sheasamh.
Coiméadaim an Tiarna
de shíor os mo choinne
agus é ar mo dheasláimh
ní chorrófar mé choíche.

2
Tá gairdeas ar mo chroí
agus áthas ar m'anam,
agus mairfidh mo cholainn
faoi shuaimhneas freisin.
Óir ní fhágfaidh tú m'anam
i measc na marbh:
ná ní ligfidh tú do do mhuirneach
truailliú a fheicéail.

3
Taispéanfaidh tú slí na beatha dom,
agus iomlán lúcháire i d'fhianaise,
agus aoibhneas ar do dheasláimh go brách.

Céad míle fáilte romhat

28

Traidisiunta

Céad míle fáilte romhat, a Íosa, a Íosa,
céad míle fáilte romhat, a Íosa.
Céad míle fáilte romhat, a Shlánaitheoir,
céad míle míle fáilte romhat, Íosa, a Íosa.
2
Glóir agus moladh duit, a Íosa, a Íosa,
glóir agus moladh duit, a Íosa.
Glóir agus moladh duit, a Shlánaitheoir,
glóir, moladh agus buíochas duit,
Íosa, a Íosa.

Christ be beside me

29

*Adapted from
'St Patrick's Breastplate'
by James Quinn, S.J.*

Christ be beside me, Christ be before me,
Christ be behind me, King of my heart.
Christ be within me, Christ be below me,
Christ be above me, never to part.
2
Christ on my right hand, Christ on my
left hand,
Christ all around me, shield in the strife.
Christ in my sleeping, Christ in my sitting,
Christ in my rising, light of my life.
3
Christ be in all hearts thinking about me.
Christ be on all tongues telling of me.
Christ be the vision in eyes that see me,
in ears that hear me, Christ ever be.

Christ is alive

30

Pamela Stotter

Christ is alive, with joy we sing:
we celebrate our risen Lord,
praising the glory of his name.
Alleluia, alleluia, alleluia.
2
He is the grain of wheat that died,
sown in distress and reaped in joy,
yielding a harvest of new life.
3
He is the sun which brings the dawn;
he is the light of all the world,
setting us free from death and sin.
4
He is the vine set in the earth,
sharing in our humanity
so we might share in God's own life.
5
He is the bread which comes from God,
broken to feed us in our need,
given to bring eternal life.
6
Christ is alive, with joy we sing;
we celebrate our risen Lord,
praising the glory of his name.

Christ be near at either hand

31

Christ be near at either hand,
Christ behind, before me stand,
Christ with me where e'er I go,
Christ around, above, below.
2
Christ be in my head and mind
Christ within my soul enshrined,
Christ control my wayward heart;
Christ abide and ne'er depart.
3
Christ my life and only way,
Christ my lantern night and day;
Christ be my unchanging friend,
Guide and shepherd to the end.
4
Christ be all my strength and might
Christ my captain for the fight;
Christ fulfil my soul's desire;
Christ ennoble and inspire.
5
Christ the King and Lord of all,
Find me ready at his call;
Christ receive my service whole
Hand and body, heart and soul.
6
Christ the King of kings descend
And of tyrants make an end;
Christ on us and all below
Concord, love and peace bestow.
7
Thanks to him, who for our food
Gives his sacred flesh and blood;
Praise to him unceasing rise
Christ whose glory fills the skies.

Críost liom
Lúireach Phádraig

32

Críost liom, Críost romham,
Críost im dhiaidh, Críost os mo chionnsa
agus Críost fúm.
Críost ina chónaí i mo chroíse,
Críost fós ó dheas díom, Críost ó thuaidh.
Ón Tiarna tig slánú, ón Tiarna tig slánú,
go raibh do shlánú a Thiarna inár measc go
saol na saol.

Clog dheá-scéal an Aingil
Brian Kelly CSSp

33

Clog dheá-scéal an Aingil, is aoibhinn a cheol.
Ag fógairt 's ag freagairt, is naofacht 'na ghlór.
Ave, Ave, Ave Maria; Ave, Ave, Ave Maria.
2
Do stiúraigh an tAingeal an cailín gan cháim,
Mar a raibh Muire Máthair os cionn
an tsrutháin.
3
Do shéid an tsí gaoithe 'na timpeall le neart,
Is tuigeadh don chailín go raibh
aoibhneas ag teacht.
4
A héadan ba ghlaine ná lile na dtonn,
Thug Bernadette grá dhi le croí is le fonn.
5
Do tháinig an tAoibhneas os comhair a dhá súl;
Bhí bean uasal álainn 'na seasamh go humhal.
6
An solas 'na timpeall, ba ghile ná'n ghrian;
De dhubhsmál an pheaca ní raibh uirthi rian.

Come adore this wondrous presence
St Thomas Aquinas (1227-74),
translated by James Quinn

34

Come, adore this wondrous presence,
bow to Christ, the source of grace.
Here is kept the ancient promise
of God's earthly dwelling-place.
Sight is blind before God's glory,
faith alone may see his face.
2
Glory be to God the Father,
praise to his co-equal Son,
adoration to the Spirit,
bond of love, in Godhead one.
Blest be God by all creation
joyously while ages run.

Come and take the flesh of Christ
Donal Murray

35

Come and take the flesh of Christ
which he gave to be our bread.
Drink the chalice of his blood
which upon the cross he shed.
2
We who are redeemed and saved
by his body and his blood,
hail the saving sacred Host
which he gave to be our food.
3
Giver of salvation,
Christ, the Son of God most high,
sacrificed to save the world,
raised with him, we will not die.

Come Christians all, rejoice and sing
36
J. Tisserand (from the Latin)

Alleluia, alleluia, alleluia.
Come, Christians all, rejoice and sing,
with thankful hearts your praises bring.
Risen is now our Lord and King.
Alleluia.
2
On Sunday morn, at break of day,
the sad disciples made their way,
seeking the place where Jesus lay.
Alleluia.
3
The Marys went, oppressed by care,
with ointments mixed with spices rare,
his blessed body to prepare.
Alleluia.
4
An angel by the tomb they see,
who speaks to them triumphantly:
'Jesus is now in Galilee.'
Alleluia.
5
Then John and Peter quickly came,
they search the tomb with hearts aflame,
his resurrection they proclaim.
Alleluia.
6
That very night, our Saviour dear
to his disciples did appear,
spoke loving words to calm their fear.
Alleluia.
7
Now let us thank the Lord most high,
and with our praises fill the sky,
for Christ is risen, no more to die.
Alleluia.

Come O Lord
37
Roger Ruston, O.P.
Based on a Jewish Passover Song

Promised Lord and Christ is he,
may we soon his kingdom see.
Come, O Lord, quickly come,
come in glory, come in glory,
come in glory, quickly come.
2
Teaching, healing once was he,
may we soon his kingdom see.
3
Dead and buried once was he,
may we soon his kingdom see.
4
Risen from the dead is he,
may we soon his kingdom see.
5
Soon to come again is he,
may we soon his kingdom see.
Come, O Lord, quickly come,
in our lifetime, in our lifetime,
in our lifetime may it be.

Come to me, Lord
38
John V. Moloney

Come to me, Lord, and live within me
Fill my soul with your life and love.

Free from sin this day, Lord, preserve me
true to your word, give me your peace.
2
Bring quick relief to all who suffer,
comfort and strength to all those who mourn.
3
You are the vine, and we the branches
though we are many, in you we are one.

Come, Holy Ghost, Creator, Come
39

Come Holy Ghost, Creator, come,
Descend from heaven's throne.
Come take possession of our hearts,
And make them all your own.
2
You are the source of strength and might,
Great gift of God above.
You are the fount of truth and light,
The flame of hope and love.
3
O Spirit promised from of old,
We offer thanks to you.
You make us live, O Lord of life,
Your power makes all things new.
4
Then come great Spirit to your own,
Our hearts make pure and strong.
Direct our weary steps today,
And turn our wills from wrong.
5
Show us the Father and the Son,
O Spirit whom they send.
That in God's kingdom we may live
The life that knows no end.
6
All glory to the Father be,
With his eternal Son,
The same unto the Paraclete,
While endless ages run.

Come, O Creator, Spirit blest 40

Come, O Creator, Spirit blest:
And in our hearts take up thy rest.
Come with thy grace and heavenly aid,
to fill the hearts which thou hast made.
2
Great Paraclete, to thee we cry,
O highest gift of God most high;
O Fount of Life, O Fire of Love,
and sweet anointing from above.
3
Thou in thy sevenfold gifts art known,
the finger of God's hand we own.
The promise of the Father, thou,
who dost the tongue with power endow.
4
Our senses kindle from above,
and make our hearts o'erflow with
love.
With patience firm and virtue high
the weakness of our flesh supply.
5
Drive far from us the foe we dread,
and grant us thy true peace instead.
So shall we not, with thee for guide,
turn from the path of life aside.
6
O may thy grace on us bestow
the Father and the Son to know,
and thee, through endless time confessed
of both, the eternal Spirit blest.
7
All glory while the ages run,
be to the Father and the Son,
who rose from death, the same to thee,
O Holy Ghost, eternally.

Come to me, all who labour 41
Weston Abbey

Come to me, all who labour and are
heavy burdened,
And I shall give you rest.
Take up my yoke and learn from me, for I am
meek and humble of heart.
And you'll find rest for your souls.
For my yoke is easy.
And my burden is light.
The Lord is my shepherd, I shall never be in need
Fresh and green are the pastures where he gives
me rest.

Day is done but love unfailing 42
James Quinn, S.J.

Day is done, but love unfailing
dwells ever here;
shadows fall, but hope, prevailing,
calms ev'ry fear.
Loving Father, none forsaking,
take our hearts, of love's own making,
watch our sleeping, guard our waking,
be always near!
2
Dark descends, but light unending
shines through our night;
you are with us, ever lending
new strength to sight;
one in love, your truth confessing,
one in hope of heaven's blessing,
may we see, in love's possessing,
love's endless light!
3
Eyes will close, but you, unsleeping,
watch by our side;
death may come: in love's safe keeping
still we abide.
God of love, all evil quelling,
sin forgiving, fear dispelling,
stay with us, our hearts indwelling,
this eventide!

Deus meus adiuva me 43
Maol Íosa Ó Brolcháin

Deus meus, adiuva me,
tabhair dom do shearc, a Mhic dhil Dé;
tabhair dom do shearc, a Mhic dhil Dé,
Deus meus adiuva me.
2
Domine, da quod peto a te,
tabhair dom go dian, a ghrian ghlan ghlé;
tabhair dom go dian, a ghrian ghlan ghlé,
Domine, da quod peto a te.
3
Tuum amorem sicut vis,
tabhair dom go tréan a déarfad arís;
tabhair dom go tréan a déarfad arís,
tuum amorem sicut vis.
4
Domine, Domine, exaudi me,
m'anam bheith lán ded'ghrá, a Dhé;
m'anam bheith lán ded'ghrá, a Dhé;
Domine, Domine, exaudi me.

Ding dong! merrily on high 44
George Ratcliffe Woodward
(1848-1934)

Ding dong! merrily on high,
in heav'n the bells are ringing;
ding dong! verily the sky
is riv'n with angels singing.

Gloria, hosanna in excelsis! (2)
2
E'en so here below, below,
let steeple bells be swungen,
and io, io, io,
by priest and people sungen.
3
Pray you, dutifully prime
your matin chime, ye ringers;
may you beautifully rime
your eventime song, ye singers.

45
Dóchas linn Naomh Pádraig
Traidisiúnta

Dóchas linn Naomh Pádraig, aspal mór na
hÉireann,
ainm oirdhearc gléigeal, solas mór an
tsaoil é.
D'fhill le soiscéal grá dúinn ainneoin
blianta 'ngéibheann.
Grá mór Mhac na páirte d'fhuascail cách
ón daorbhroid.
2
Sléibhte, gleannta, maighe's bailte mór' na
hÉireann:
ghlan sé iad go deo dúinn, míle glóir dár
naomh dhil.
Iarr'mid ort, a Phádraig, guí orainn na
Gaela.
Dia linn lá 'gus oíche's Pádraig aspal
Éireann.

46
Fáilte romhat, a Rí na nAingeal
Traidisiúnta

Fáilte romhat, a Rí na n-aingeal,
t'réis do ghlactha, a choirp an Rí;
Fáilte romhat, a Rí na bhflaitheas,
Fóir, a Chríost, gach duine dínn.
Glóir don Athair, don Mhac 's don Naoimh
Sprid.
Glóir go deo is moladh síor.
2
Dia do bheatha, a Thiarna Dia,
Dia is duine thú, a Íosa Críost;
Dia do bheatha, 'bhláth is gile,
Tusa beatha chách go fíor.
Glóir don Athair . . .
3
Dia do bheatha, 'bhláth na lile,
'Aon-Mhic Mhuire, a ghin gan smál;
Dia do bheatha, 'chroí is glaine,
D'fhuascail sinn led chrois 's led pháis.
Glóir don Athair . . .

47
For all the saints
William Walsham How (1823-97)

For all the saints
who from their labours rest,
who their great faith
to all the world confest,
your name, O Jesus,
be for ever blest.
Alleluia, alleluia.
2
You were their rock,
their fortress and their might,
their valiant captain
in the well-fought fight,
and in the darkness
their unfailing light.
3
May all the faithful,
joined within one fold,
strive as the saints
who bravely fought of old,
and win, like them,
the victor's crown of gold.

4
O blest communion,
fellowship divine,
we feebly struggle,
they in glory shine,
yet all in Christ unite,
in him combine.
5
And when the strife is fierce,
the struggle long,
then from the distance
sounds the triumph song,
and hearts are bold again
and courage strong.
6
The golden evening
brightens in the west,
soon to the steadfast
faithful comes their rest:
the soothing calm
of Paradise so blest.
7
But still there breaks
a far more glorious day,
the saints triumphant
rise in bright array,
the King of glory
passes on his way.
8
From earth's wide bounds,
from ocean's furthest coast,
through gates of glory
streams the countless host,
and sings to Father,
Son and Holy Ghost.

48
Gabham molta Bhríde

Gabham molta Bhríde,
Ionúin í le hÉireann,
Ionúin le gach tír í,
Molaimís go léir í.
2
Lóchrann geal na Laighneach
'soilsiú feadh na tíre.
Ceann ar ógha Éireann,
Ceann na mban ar míne.
3
Tig an geimhreadh dian dubh
'Gearradh lena ghéire;
Ach ar lá 'le Bríde
Gar dúinn earrach Éireann.

Gift of finest wheat
O. Westendorf

49

*You satisfy the hungry heart with gift
of finest wheat;
Come give to us, O saving Lord, the bread
of life to eat.*

As when the shepherd calls his sheep
They know and heed his voice;
So when you call your fam'ly Lord,
we follow and rejoice.
2
With joyful lips we sing to you
Our praise and gratitude,
That you should count us worthy, Lord,
To share this heavenly food.
3
Is not the cup we bless and share
The blood of Christ outpoured?
Do not one cup, one loaf, declare
Our oneness in the Lord?
4
You give yourself to us. O Lord:
Then selfless let us be,
To serve each other in your name
In truth and charity.

Gile mo chroí
Tadhg Gaelach Ó Súilleabháin

50

Gile mo chroí do chroíse 'Shlánaitheoir,
Is ciste mo chroí do chroíse d'fháil im
chomhair,
Ós follas gur líon do chroí dom' ghrásta 'stór,
I gcochall mo chroí do chroíse fág i gcomhad.
2
Ar fhulaingis trínne a Rí ghil ard na gcomhacht,
Ní thigeann im smaointe a shuíomh ná
a thrácht i gcóir;

'S gur le goradhghoin nimhe do chroí's do
chneása, a stór,
Do bhrostaigh na mílte saoi go sámh i gcoróin.
3
A Athair 's a Íosa dhíon led bhás mé beo,
'S do dhealbh mo ghnaoi gan chríochnú ceard
id chló,
Nach danartha an gníomh, a Chríost, nár
ghrása fós
Ach gach uile ní 'na mbíodh do ghráin
don tsórt.

Glory to you, my God, this night

51

Glory to you, my God, this night
for all the blessings of the light;
O keep me, Lord, great King of kings,
beneath your own almighty wings.
2
Forgive me, Lord, by your dear Son,
the ill that I this day have done,
so that within your grace I keep
and be at peace before I sleep.
3
Teach me to live, that I may dread
my grave as little as my bed;
teach me to die, that so I may
rise glorious at the Final Day.
4
O may my soul in you repose,
and with sweet sleep mine eyelids close,
a sleep that I may vigour take
to serve my God when I awake.
5
Praise God, from whom all blessings flow;
praise him, all creatures here below;
praise him above, great heav'nly host;
praise Father, Son and Holy Ghost.

God full of mercy
Lucien Deiss.

52

*God, full of mercy and God of compassion;
God, rich in kindness and faithful in your love;
God, who grants pardon to those who seek you,
and who treasure your living Word.*

God of tenderness and love,
you, Lord are my Saviour!
God, my courage and my strength:
you, Lord, are my love;
reveal your name to me;
show me the light of your face.
2
Lord, your mercy fills the earth,
you, Lord are my Saviour.
Lord, you pardon all my sins:
you, Lord, are my love;
reveal your name to me;
show me the light of your face.
3
God the Father of the poor:
you, Lord, are my Saviour.
God, protector of the weak:
you, Lord, are my love;
reveal your name to me;
show me the light of your face.
4
God, who calls all men to life:
you, Lord, are my Saviour.
God, who knows us by our name:
you, Lord, are my love;
reveal your name to me;
show me the light of your face.
5
God, the Mystery of light:
you, Lord, are my Saviour.
God, revealed through Christ, your Son:
you, Lord, are my love;
reveal your name to me;
show me the light of your face.

God of mercy and compassion **53**
E. Vaughan (1827-1908)

God of mercy and compassion,
look with pity upon me;
Father, let me call thee Father,
'tis thy child returns to thee.
Jesus Lord, I ask for mercy;
let me not implore in vain;
all my sins I now detest them,
never will I sin again.
2
See our Saviour, bleeding, dying,
on the cross of Calvary;
to that cross my sins have nail'd him,
yet he bleeds and dies for me.

God of mercy and compassion **54**
New alternative text
by Michael Hodgetts

God of mercy and compassion,
Lord of life and blinding light.
Truth whom creatures would refashion,
force on us the gift of sight.
Truth insistent and demanding,
love resented and ignored;
life beyond all understanding,
give us peace and pardon, Lord.
2
God most holy and forgiving,
penetrate our pride and sloth:
On a people partly living
force the gift of life and growth.
3
Lord, who out of love consented
to the worst mankind could do,
Lord abandoned and tormented,
let us love and suffer too.

Grant to us, O Lord **55**
Lucien Deiss (based on Ez 36:26
and Jer 31:31-34)

Grant to us, O Lord, a heart renewed;
recreate in us your own Spirit, Lord!

Behold the days are coming
says the Lord our God
when I will make a new covenant
with the house of Israel.
2
Deep within their being
I will implant my law;
I will write it on their hearts.
3
I will be their God,
and they shall be my people.
4
And for all their faults
I will grant forgiveness;
nevermore will I remember their sins.

God's blessing sends us forth **56**
J. C. Evers

God's blessing sends us forth,
strengthened for our task on earth,
refreshed in soul, renewed in mind.
May God with us remain,
through us his Spirit reign
that Christ be known to all mankind.
2
God's news in spoken word
joyfully our hearts have heard;
O may the seed of God's love now grow.
May we in fruitful deeds
gladly serve others' needs
that faith in action we may show.

3
We by one living bread
as one body have been fed,
so we are one in true brotherhood;
how gracious to behold
all brethren of one fold
who ever seek each other's good.
4
Grant to our restless race
triumph of your truth and grace;
Lord, you alone are unchanging truth.
Preserve and ever guide,
as your fair spotless bride,
your ancient Church in ageless youth.

Hail Glorious St. Patrick **57**
Sister Agnes

Hail, glorious Saint Patrick,
dear saint of our isle
on us thy poor children
bestow a sweet smile;
and now thou art high
in the mansions above,
on Erin's green valleys
look down in thy love.
On Erin's green valleys (3)
look down in thy love.
2
Ever bless and defend the sweet
land of our birth,
where the shamrock still blooms
as when thou wert on earth,
our hearts shall yet burn,
wheresoever we roam,
for God and Saint Patrick,
and our native home.

Hail Queen of Heaven
John Lingard (1771-1851) **58**

Hail, Queen of heav'n, the ocean star,
guide of the wand'rer here below;
thrown on life's surge, we claim thy care;
save us from peril and from woe.
Mother of Christ, star of the sea,
pray for the wanderer, pray for me.

2
O gentle, chaste and spotless maid,
we sinners make our prayers through thee;
remind thy Son that he has paid
the price of our iniquity.
Virgin most pure, star of the sea,
pray for the sinner, pray for me.

3
Sojourners in this vale of tears,
to thee, blest advocate, we cry;
pity our sorrows, calm our fears,
and soothe with hope our misery.
Refuge in grief, star of the sea,
pray for the mourner, pray for me.

4
And while to him who reigns above,
in Godhead One, in Persons Three,
the source of life, of grace, of love,
homage we pay on bended knee,
do thou, bright Queen, star of the sea,
pray for thy children, pray for me.

Hail, Redeemer, King divine!
Patrick Brennan (1877-1952) **59**

Hail, Redeemer, King divine!
Priest and Lamb, the throne is thine,
King, whose reign shall never cease,
Prince of everlasting peace.

Angels, saints and nations sing:
'Praised be Jesus Christ, our King;
Lord of life, earth, sky and sea,
King of love on Calvary.'

2
King whose name creation thrills,
rule our minds, our hearts, our wills,
till in peace each nation rings
with thy praises. King of kings.

3
King most holy, King of truth,
guide the lowly, guide the youth;
Christ, thou King of glory bright,
be to us eternal light.

4
Shepherd-King, o'er mountains steep,
homeward bring the wandering sheep,
shelter in one royal fold
states and kingdoms, new and old.

Hail to the Lord who comes
J. Ellerton **60**

Hail to the Lord who comes,
Comes to his temple gate.
Not with his angel hosts
not in his kingly state.

But borne upon the throne
Of Mary's gentle breast:
Thus to his Father's house
He comes, a humble guest.

3
The world's true light draws near
All darkness to dispel.
The flame of faith is lit
And dies the power of hell.

4
Our bodies and our souls
Are temples now for him,
For we are born of grace—
God lights our souls within.

5
O Light of all the earth!
We light our lives with thee;
The chains of darkness gone
All sons of God are free.

Hark, the herald angels sing
C. Wesley (1743), G. Whitefield
(1753), M. Madan (1760),
and others **61**

Hark, the herald angels sing,
glory to the new-born King;
peace on earth and mercy mild,
God and sinners reconciled;
joyful all ye nations rise,
join the triumph of the skies,
with the angelic host proclaim.
Christ is born in Bethlehem.

Hark, the herald Angels sing,
glory to the new-born King.

2
Christ, by highest heaven adored,
Christ, the everlasting Lord,
late in time behold him come,
offspring of the Virgin's womb!
Veiled in flesh the Godhead see,
hail the incarnate Deity!
Pleased as man with us to dwell,
Jesus, our Emmanuel.

3
Hail the heaven-born Prince of peace!
Hail the Son of righteousness!
Light and life to all he brings
risen with healing in his wings;
mild he lays his glory by;
born that we no more may die,
born to raise us from the earth,
born to give us second birth.

Heart of Christ, we sing your praises
M. Farrell

62

Heart of Christ we sing your praises,
Wellspring of eternal life.
Through the sorrows of your passion
we find refuge from our strife.
2
Heart of Christ, that now embodies
All the wonder of God's love,
You tell us the tender mercies,
Showered from our God above.
3
Heart of Christ, who brings all healing
To the lowly and the weak,
Let us know your loving kindness,
Show yourself to all who seek.

Holy Spirit Lord of Love

63

Holy Spirit Lord of love,
Wisdom coming from above.
Gifts of blessing to bestow,
On your waiting Church below.
Once again in love draw near,
To your people gathered here.
Since our great baptismal day,
You have led us on your way.
2
You have been our constant guide,
ever watching by our side.
May we now 'till life shall end,
Choose and know you as our friend.
Give us life to live for you;
Give us love, forever new.
Come then, Holy Spirit, come;
Make each heart your happy home.

Holy God we praise thy name
C.A. Walworth (1820-1900)

64

Holy God, we praise thy name,
Lord of all, we bow before thee.
All on earth thy sceptre own,
all in heaven above adore thee.
Endless is thy vast domain,
everlasting is thy reign.
2
Hark, with loud and pealing hymn,
thee the angel choirs are praising;
cherubim and seraphim,
one unceasing chorus raising,
ever sing with sweet accord,
holy, holy, holy Lord.
3
Spare thy people, Lord, we pray,
by a thousand snares surrounded:
keep us free from sin today;
never let us be confounded.
All my trust I place in thee;
never, Lord abandon me.
4
Holy Father, Holy Son,
Holy Spirit, three we name thee,
While in essence only one,
Undivided God, we claim thee.
And adoring, bend the knee,
while we own the mystery.

I am the bread of life
Sister Suzanne Toolan, S.M.

65

I am the Bread of Life. You who come to
me shall not hunger,
and who believe in me shall not thirst.
No one can come to me unless
the Father beckon.
*And I will raise you up, and I will raise you up,
and I will raise you up on the last day.*

2
The bread that I will give is my flesh
for the life of the world,
and if you eat of this bread,
you shall live forever,
you shall live forever.
3
Unless you eat of the flesh of the Son of Man
and drink of his blood, and drink of his blood,
you shall not have life within you.
4
I am the Resurrection, I am the life.
If you believe in me, even though you die,
you shall live forever.
5
Yes, Lord, I believe that you are the Christ,
the Son of God who have come into the world.

I'll sing a hymn to Mary
F. Wyse–D. Murray

66

I'll sing a hymn to Mary,
the mother of my God,
the virgin of all virgins,
of David's royal blood.
*O holy mother Mary,
ask Christ your Son we pray
to grant us his forgiveness,
and guide us on his way.*
2
Rejoice, O holy Mary,
O Virgin full of grace,
the Lord is ever with you,
most blessed of our race.

In faith and hope and love

67

In faith and hope and love,
with joyful trust we move
towards our Father's home above.
Christ our star, our guide, our road
To the Father's high abode.
2
Christ our bread along the way,
Christ our rescue when we stray.
3
Christ our shelter, Christ our friend,
Our beginning and our end.
4
Christ our hope and our reward,
Our Redeemer and our Lord.

Into one we are all gathered

68

Adapted from "Ubi Caritas et Amor"
by Michael Cockett

Into one we are all gathered
through the love of Christ.
Let us then rejoice with gladness,
in him we find love.
Let us fear and love the living God,
and love and cherish all mankind.
Where charity and love are, there is God.
2
Therefore, when we are together
in the love of Christ,
let us then minds know no division,
strife or bitterness;
may the Christ our God be in our midst.
Through Christ our Lord all love is found.
3
May we see your face in glory,
Christ our loving God.
With the blessed saints of heaven
give us lasting joy.
We will then possess true happiness,
and love for all eternity.

I place all my trust in you, my God

69

Psalm 129 (The Grail)

I place all my trust in you, my God:
all my hope is in your saving Word.

Out of the depths I cry to you, O Lord,
Lord, hear my voice!
O let your ears be attentive
to the voice of my pleading.
2
If you, O Lord, should mark our guilt,
Lord, who would survive?
But with you is found forgiveness:
for this we revere you.
3
My soul is waiting for the Lord,
I count on his word.
My soul is longing for the Lord
more than watchman for daybreak.
4
Because with the Lord there is mercy
and fullness of redemption.
Israel indeed he will redeem
from all its iniquity.
5
To the Father Almighty give glory,
give glory to his Son,
to the Spirit most Holy give praise,
whose reign is for ever.

Is maith an bhean Muire mhór

70

Traidisiúnta

Is maith an bhean Muire mhór,
Máthair Ard-Rí na slógh síor;
siad a grásta is gnáth lán,
bean do chuir fál fó gach tír.
2
Bean í dá gclaonann ceart,
bean is mó neart is brí,
bean is boige fá ór dearg,
bean le gcoistear fearg an Rí.

3
Bean do bheir radharc do dhall,
bean is treise thall ar neamh,
bean do thóg mo naimhde díom,
bean is díon dom as gach cath.

Jesus and Mary be your guests this hour

71

Sister Margarita

Jesus and Mary be your guests this hour,
As once they came to bless the marriage
feast,
Making you share Christ's consecrating power,
Each for the other sacramental priest.
2
Peace be within you, and the joy today
Spring up anew, though human life be frail.
Our Lord sustain you with his grace we pray.
His faithful love, good wine that cannot fail.

Jesus Christ is risen today

72

Lyra Davidica (1708) and
the Supplement (1816)

Jesus Christ is risen today, alleluia!
Our triumphant holy day, alleluia!
Who did once, upon the cross, alleluia!
Suffer to redeem our loss, alleluia!
2
Hymns of praise then let us sing, alleluia!
Unto Christ, our heavenly king, alleluia!
Who endured the cross and grave, alleluia!
Sinners to redeem and save, alleluia!
3
But the pains that he endured, alleluia!
Our salvation have procured; alleluia!
Now above the sky he's king, alleluia!
Where the angels ever sing, alleluia!

Keep in mind
Lucien Deiss

73

Keep in mind that Jesus Christ has died for us
and is risen from the dead.
He is our saving Lord, he is joy for all ages.

If we die with the Lord,
we shall live with the Lord.
2
If we endure with the Lord,
we shall reign with the Lord.
3
In him all our sorrow, in him all our joy.
4
In him hope of glory, in him all our love.
5
In him our redemption, in him all our grace.
6
In him our salvation, in him all our peace.

Jesus my Lord, my God my all
Frederick William Faber (1814-63)

74

Jesus, my Lord, my God, my all,
how can I love thee as I ought?
And how revere this wondrous gift
so far surpassing hope or thought?

Sweet Sacrament, we thee adore;
Oh, make us love thee more and more.

2
Had I but Mary's sinless heart
to love thee with, my dearest King,
Oh, with what bursts of fervent praise
thy goodness, Jesus, would I sing!
3
Ah, see! within a creature's hand
the vast Creator deigns to be,
reposing, infant-like, as though
on Joseph's arm, or Mary's knee.

4
Thy body, soul, and Godhead, all;
O mystery of love divine!
I cannot compass all I have,
for all thou hast and art are mine.
5
Sound, sound, his praises higher still,
and come, ye angels, to our aid;
'tis God, 'tis God, the very God
whose power both man and angels made.

Laudate Dominum
Psalm 116

75

Adoremus in aeternum,
sanctissimum Sacramentum.

Laudate Dominum, omnes gentes,
laudate eum omnes populi.
2
Quoniam confirmata est super nos
misericordia ejus;
et veritas Domini manet in aeternum.
3
Gloria Patri, et Filio et Spiritui Sancto.
4
Sicut erat in principio, et nunc et semper,
et in saecula saeculorum. Amen.

Let me sing of your law
Lucien Deiss

76

Let me sing of your law, O my God.
Let your love come upon your people.

Through your own word, Lord, give us life.
In your holy keeping, happy is my soul.
2
Show me the way to keep your law.
Let your holy precepts dwell within my mind.
3
O take me far from evil ways,
and in your great mercy guide me in your paths.

4
Within your law I choose to live.
In the paths of wisdom I walk evermore.
5
My heart is strong, my joy is full.
Following your law, Lord, freely do I walk.

Let not your hearts be troubled
Author unknown. Based on Jn.14.

77

Let not your hearts be troubled,
you believe in God,
believe also in me.
In my Father's house are many mansions,
if it were not so, would I have told you?
2
I go to prepare a place for you,
and when I go and prepare a place for you,
I will come again and take you to myself,
that where I am, there you may be also.

Let the earth rejoice and sing
Melvin Farrell

78

Let the earth rejoice and sing, alleluia,
at the triumph of our King, alleluia.
He ascends from mortal sight, alleluia,
reigns now at our Father's right, alleluia.
2
He who died upon a tree, alleluia,
now shall reign eternally, alleluia.
He who saved our fallen race, alleluia,
takes in heav'n his rightful place, alleluia.
3
Jesus, victor, hear our prayer, alleluia.
In thy triumph let us share, alleluia.
Lift our minds and hearts above, alleluia.
Strengthen all men in thy love, alleluia.
4
While in heaven thou dost gaze, alleluia,
on thy Church who sings thy praise, alleluia,
fasten all our hope in thee, alleluia,
till thy face unveiled we see, alleluia.

Listen to the Word
Margaret Daly.
(Based on the prologue to the
Rule of St Benedict and Psalm 118)

79

Open your eyes to the light!
Open your ears to the word!
Today if you hear his voice,
harden not your hearts,
but listen! listen to the living Word of God.

Open my eyes that I may see the wonders of
your law.
Guide me in the path of your commands,
for there is my delight.
Hear the voice of the Lord inviting us:
behold in his loving kindness he shows us the
path of life.
2
Your will is wonderful indeed, therefore I obey it.
See how I love your precepts,
in your mercy give me life.
Hear the voice of the Lord inviting us:
behold in his loving kindness he shows us the
path of life.
3
Lord, let my cry come before you;
teach me by your word.
I long for your saving help.
Your law is my delight.
Hear the voice of the Lord inviting us:
behold in his loving kindness he shows us the
path of life.
4
Lord, how I love your law;
it is always in my mind.
Your promise is sweeter to my taste than honey
in the mouth.
Hear the voice of the Lord inviting us:
behold in his loving kindness he shows us the
path of life.

5
I rejoice to do your will,
as though all riches were mine.
I will run in the way of your commands;
you give freedom to my heart.
Hear the voice of the Lord inviting us:
behold in his loving kindness he shows us the
path of life.
6
Let your face shine on your servant,
teach me your decrees.
The justice of your will is eternal:
if you teach me I shall live.
Hear the voice of the Lord inviting us:
behold in his loving kindness he shows us the
path of life.

Like the deer that yearns
Psalm 41:1, 42:3-4 (Joseph Walshe)

80

Like the deer that yearns for running
streams
so my soul is yearning for you, my God.

My soul is thirsting for God,
the God of my life.
When can I enter and see
the face of God?
2
O send forth your light and your truth,
let these be my guide.
Let them bring me to your holy mountain,
to the place where you dwell.
3
And I will come to the altar of God,
the God of my joy,
my redeemer, I will thank you on the harp,
O God, my God.

Lord accept the gifts we offer
Sister M. Teresine

81

Lord accept the gifts we offer
at this Eucharistic feast,
bread and wine to be transformed now
through the action of thy priest
take us too, Lord, and transform us,
be thy grace in us increased.
2
May our souls be pure and spotless
as the host of wheat so fine;
may all stain of sin be crushed out,
like the grape that forms the wine,
as we, too, become partakers,
in this sacrifice divine.
3
Take our gifts, almighty Father,
living God, eternal, true,
which we give through Christ our Saviour,
pleading here for us anew.
Grant salvation to all present.
and our faith and love renew.

Lord dismiss us with your blessing
Author unknown

82

Lord, dismiss us with your blessing;
fill our hearts with joy and peace.
Let us each, your love possessing,
in our love for you increase.
Come, Lord Jesus, and refresh us,
from our sins grant us relief.
2
Thanks we give and adoration
for the Gospel's joyful sound.
May the fruits of your salvation
in our hearts and lives abound.
May your everlasting presence
with us evermore be found.

83

Lord, let your face shine on us.
Psalm 4.

Lord, let your face shine on us.
When I call, answer me, O God of justice;
from anguish you release me,
have mercy and hear me.
2
O men, how long will your hearts be closed,
will you love what is futile and seek what is false?
3
It is the Lord who grants favours to those
whom he loves;
the Lord hears me whenever I call him.
4
Fear him; do not sin:
ponder on your bed and be still.
Make justice your sacrifice and trust in the Lord.
5
"What can bring us happiness?" many say.
Let the light of your face shine on us, O Lord.
6
You have put into my heart a greater joy
than they have from abundance of corn and
new wine.

84

Lord of all hopefulness
Jan Struther (1901-53)

Lord of all hopefulness.
Lord of all joy,
whose trust, ever child-like,
no cares could destroy,
be there at our waking,
and give us, we pray,
your bliss in our hearts, Lord,
at the break of the day.
2
Lord of all eagerness,
Lord of all faith,
whose strong hands were skilled
at the plane and the lathe,
be there at our labours,
and give us, we pray,
your strength in our hearts, Lord,
at the noon of the day.
3
Lord of all kindliness,
Lord of all grace,
your hands swift to welcome,
your arms to embrace,
be there at our homing,
and give us, we pray,
your love in our hearts, Lord,
at the eve of the day.
4
Lord of all gentleness,
Lord of all calm,
whose voice is contentment,
whose presence is balm,
be there at our sleeping,
and give us, we pray,
your peace in our hearts, Lord,
at the end of the day.

85

Loving shepherd of thy sheep

Loving shepherd of thy sheep,
Keep me, Lord, in safety keep;
Nothing can thy power withstand,
None can pluck me from thy hand.
Loving shepherd thou did'st give
Thine own life that I might live;
May I love thee day by day,
Gladly thy sweet will obey.
2
Loving shepherd ever near,
Teach me still thy voice to hear;
Suffer not my step to stray,
From the straight and narrow way.
Where thou leadest may I go,
Walking in thy steps below;
Then before thy father's throne,
Jesus, claim me for thine own.

86

Love is his word
Luke Connaughton (1916-79)

Love is his word, love is his way,
feasting with men, fasting alone,
living and dying, rising again,
love, only love, is his way.
Richer than gold
is the love of my Lord;
better than splendour and wealth.
2
Love is his way, love is his mark,
sharing his last Passover feast,
Christ at this table, host to the Twelve.
Love, only love, is his mark.
3
Love is his mark, love is his sign,
bread for our strength, wine for our joy
'This is my body, this is my blood.'
Love, only love, is his sign.
4
Love is his sign, love is his news,
'Do this,' he said 'lest you forget
all my deep sorrow, all my dear blood.'
love, only love, is his news.
5
Love is his news, love is his name,
we are his own, chosen and called,
family, brethren, cousins and kin.
Love, only love, is his name.
6
Love is his name, love is his law.
Hear his command, all who are his:
'Love one another, I have love you.'
Love, only love, is his law.
7
Love is his law, love is his word:
love of the Lord, Father and Word,
love of the Spirit, God ever one,
love, only love, is his word.

Maranatha.
Lucien Deiss.

87

Maranatha! Come, O Christ the Lord.

I am the root of Jesse and David's Son,
the radiant star of morning and God's own light.
2
The Spirit and the Bride say: "Come".
Let him who hears their voices say: "Come".
3
He who has thirst let him come,
and he who has desire, let him drink
the waters of everlasting life.
4
"Yes, I come very soon,"
Amen. Come, O Lord Jesus.

Make me a channel of your peace
Sebastian Temple

88

Make me a channel of your peace.
Where there is hatred, let me bring your
love.
Where there is injury, your pardon, Lord.
And where there's doubt, true faith in you.
2
Make me a channel of your peace.
Where there's despair in life, let me bring
hope.
Where there is darkness only light,
and where there's sadness ever joy.
3
Oh, Master, grant that I may never seek
so much to be consoled as to console,
to be understood as to understand,
to be loved, as to love, with all my soul.
4
Make me a channel of your peace.
It is in pardoning that we are pardoned,
in giving to all men that we receive,
and in dying that we're born to eternal life.

May Christ live in our hearts
Sr Suzanne Toolan

89

May Christ live in our hearts, through faith
may he be with us,
that planted and built on love, we may
proclaim his goodness.
Glory be to him whose power is at work in us.
Praise God the father of Our Lord Jesus Christ.
2
For this we pray to the Father, that he may
give us power,
in his Spirit that we may grow in love and
inner strength.
3
With courage then in our prayer we approach
the Lord in trust,
for we are God's work, a temple to his glory.
4
May we stand firm in the truth, hold fast the
shield of faith,
proclaim the Gospel of peace in eager
honest deeds.

May flights of angels

90

May flights of angels lead you on your way
To paradise, and heaven's eternal day!
May martyrs greet you after death's dark night,
And bid you enter into Sion's light!
May choirs of angels sing you to your rest
With once poor Lazarus, now for ever blest!

May your love be upon us O Lord
Psalm 32 (Margaret Daly)

91

May your love be upon us, O Lord,
as we place all our hope in you.

For the word of the Lord is faithful,
and all his works to be trusted.
The Lord loves justice and right,
and fills the earth with his love.
2
The Lord looks on those who revere him,
on those who hope in his love,
to rescue their souls from death,
to keep them alive in famine.
3
Our soul is waiting for the Lord;
the Lord is our help and our shield,
in him do our hearts find joy;
we trust in his holy name.

Molaigí an Tiarna
Salm 116 (Kevin Healey O.S.B.)

92

Molaigí an Tiarna, alleluia!

Molaigí an Tiarna, a chiníocha go léir,
alleluia.
Molaigí É, a náisiúin uile.
2
Óir bíonn carthanacht trócaireach dúinn
ag dul i méid i gcónaí,
alleluia.
Agus maireann fírinne an Tiarna go deo.

Móradh duit a Rí na cruinne
Baile an Fhirtéaraigh

93

Móradh duit a Rí na cruinne,
maidin Domhnaigh inár ndáil;
móradh duit, a Dhia 's a dhuine,
moladh's glóire duit go brách.
2
Moladh 's glóire, moladh 's glóire,
moladh 's buíochas duit is grá,
moladh 's glóire, moladh 's glóire.
's moladh ó shlóite cheithre ard.

Morning has broken
Eleanor Farjeon (1881-1965)

94

Morning has broken like the first morning,
blackbird has spoken like the first bird.
Praise for the singing! Praise for the
morning!
Praise for them, springing fresh from the
Word!
2
Sweet the rain's new fall sunlit from heaven,
like the first dew-fall on the first grass.
Praise for the sweetness of the wet garden,
sprung in completeness where his feet pass.
3
Mine is the sunlight! Mine is the morning
born of the one light Eden saw play!
Praise with elation, praise ev'ry morning,
God's re-creation of the new day!

My God accept my heart this day
Matthew Bridges (1800-94)

95

My God, accept my heart this day,
and make it wholly thine,
that I from thee no more may stray,
no more from thee decline.
2
Before the cross of him who died,
behold, I prostrate fall;
let every sin be crucified,
and Christ be all in all.
3
Anoint me with thy heavenly grace,
and seal me for thine own,
that I may see thy glorious face,
and worship at thy throne.
4
Let every thought, and work and word
to thee be ever given,
then life shall be thy service, Lord,
and death the gate of heaven.
5
All glory to the Father be,
all glory to the Son,
all glory, Holy Ghost, to thee
while endless ages run.

My soul is longing for your peace
Lucien Deiss (based on Psalm 131)

96

*My soul is longing for your peace,
near to you, my God*
Lord, you know that my heart is not proud,
and my eyes are not lifted from the earth.
2
Lofty thoughts have never filled my mind,
far beyond my sight all ambitious deeds.
3
In your peace I have maintained my soul,
I have kept my heart in your quiet peace.

4
As a child rests on his mother's knee,
so I place my soul in your loving care.
5
Israel, put all your hope in God,
place your trust in him, now and evermore.

Nearer my God to thee
Sarah Flower Adams (1805-48)

97

Nearer my God to thee, nearer to thee,
e'en though it be a cross that raiseth me;
still all my song shall be nearer my God
to thee,
nearer my God to thee, nearer to thee.
2
Though like the wanderer, the sun
gone down,
darkness be over me, my rest a stone;
yet in my dreams I'd be nearer my God
to thee,
nearer my God to thee, nearer to thee.
3
There let the way appear steps unto heav'n
all that thou sendest me in mercy giv'n;
angels to beckon me nearer my God to thee
nearer my God to thee, nearer to thee.
4
Deep in thy sacred heart let me abide,
thou who hast come for me, suffered
and died.
Sweet shall my weeping be, grief surely
leading me
nearer my God to thee, nearer to thee.

Now thank we all our God
Martin Rinkart (1586-1649)
tr. Catherine Winkworth

98

Now thank we all our God,
with heart and hand and voices,
who wondrous things has done,
in whom this world rejoices;
who from our mother's arms
has blessed us on our way
with countless gifts of love,
and still is ours today.

2
O may this bounteous God
through all our lives be near us,
with ever joyful hearts
and blessed peace to cheer us;
and keep us in his grace,
and guide us when perplexed,
and free us from all ills
in this world and the next.

3
All praise and thanks to God
the Father now be given,
the Son and Spirit blest
who reign in highest heaven,
the one Eternal God,
whom earth and heaven adore;
for thus it was, is now,
and shall be evermore.

Now the green blade rises
J.M.C. Crum (1872-1958)

99

Now the green blade rises
from the buried grain,
wheat that in dark earth
many days has lain.
Love lives again,
that with the dead has been:
Love is come again.
like wheat that springs up green.

2
In the grave they laid him,

Love whom men had slain,
thinking that never
he would wake again,
laid in the earth
like grain that sleeps unseen:
Love is come again
like wheat that springs up green.

3
Forth he came at Easter,
like the risen grain,
he that for three days
in the grave had lain,
quick from the dead
my risen Lord is seen:
Love is come again
like wheat that springs up green.

4
When our hearts are wintry,
grieving, or in pain,
your touch can call us back
to life again,
fields of our hearts
that dead and bare have been:
Love is come again
like wheat that springs up green

O come all ye faithful
(18th cent) tr. F. Oakeley

100

O come, all ye faithful,
joyful and triumphant,
O come ye, O come ye to Bethlehem;
come and behold him,
born the king of angels:
O come, let us adore him, (3)
Christ the Lord.

2
Born of the father,
Light from light eternal,
Son of the gentle maid,
our flesh and blood.
Honour and praise him
with the hosts of angels.

3
Sing, choirs of angels,
sing in exultation,
sing all ye citizens of heaven above;
glory to God
in the highest:

4
Now, Lord, we greet you,
born this happy morning,
Jesus, to you be glory given;
Word of the Father,
now in flesh appearing:

O comfort my people
Chrysogonous Waddell
(based on Isaiah 40)

101

O comfort my people
and calm all their fear,
and tell them the time
of salvation draws near.
O tell them I come
to remove all their shame.
Then they will for ever
give praise to my name.

2
Proclaim to the cities
of Juda my word;
that 'gentle yet strong
is the hand of the Lord.
I rescue the captives,
my people defend,
and bring them to justice
and joy without end'.

3
'All mountains and hills
shall become as a plain,
for vanished are mourning
and hunger and pain,
and never again
shall these war against you.
Behold I come quickly,
to make all things new.'

O come, O come, Emmanuel

102

O come, O come Emmanuel
and ransom captive Israel
that mourns in lonely exile here
until the Son of God appear.
Rejoice, rejoice, O Israel,
to you shall come Emmanuel
2
O come now, Wisdom from on high
who orders all things mightily.
To us, the path of knowledge show
and teach us in Her ways to go.
3
O come, O come Great Lord of Might,
who once appeared on Sinai's height,
and gave your faithful people Law.
In all the splendour we adore.
4
O Royal Branch of Jesse's Tree
redeem us all from tyranny;
from pain of hell your people free
and over death win victory.
5
O Key of David's City, come
and open wide our heavenly home:
Make safe the way that leads above;
protect us ever by your love.
6
O come Great Day-Star, radiance bright,
and heal us with your glorious light.
Disperse the gloomy clouds of night
and death's dark shadows put to flight.
7
O come Desire of Nations, bind
in one the hearts of all mankind.
Bid now our sad divisions cease
and be yourself our King of Peace.

O Cross of Christ immortal tree
Stanbrook Abbey Nuns

103

O Cross of Christ, immortal tree
on which our Saviour died,
the world is sheltered by your arms
that bore the Crucified.
2
From bitter death and barren wood
the tree of life is made;
its branches bear unfailing fruit
and leaves that never fade.
3
O faithful Cross, you stand unmoved
while ages run their course;
foundation of the universe,
creation's binding force.
4
Give glory to the risen Christ
and to his Cross give praise,
the sign of God's unfathomed love,
the hope of all our days.

O help of Christians, Mother dear
P.J. Brennan

104

O help of Christians, Mother dear,
Thy children cry to thee.
From lonely homes where sorrow's tear,
Is bitter as the sea.
O Queen of Peace, to thee we pray,
That ruthless war may cease.
That all may sing,
Hail Christ our King!
Hail full of grace! –
Hail Queen of peace.
2
True Queen of prophets, who foretold,
The prince of peace and love,
Inspire all nations, young and old,
With wisdom from above.

3
Bright Queen of angels while we sing
glad tidings of God's birth,
implore for us, from Christ our King,
good will and peace on earth.
4
True Queen of Martyrs, as you trod
the path to Calvary,
restore the fruitful peace of God:
truth, justice, charity.

Oíche chiúin

105

Oíche chiúin, oíche Mhic Dé,
Cách 'na suan go héirí an lae.
Dís is dílse ag faire le spéis.
Glór binn aingeal le clos ins an aer.
Críost ag teacht ar an saol.
Críost ag teacht ar an saol.
2
Oíche chiúin, oíche Mhic Dé,
Aoirí ar dtús a chuala an scéal.
Alleluia aingeal ag glaoch,
Cantain suairc i ngar is i gcéin.
Críost ár Slánaitheoir féin
Críost ár Slánaitheoir féin.

O sacrament most holy
Traditional

106

O sacrament most holy,
O sacrament divine,
all praise and all thanksgiving
be ev'ry moment thine.

O Lord I am not worthy
107

O Lord I am not worthy,
To house thee in my soul.
One word all powerful from thee
Will make me clean and whole.

2
O sacrament most holy,
O sacrament divine,
All praise and all thanksgiving
Be ev'ry moment thine.

O king of might and splendour
Dom Gregory Murray, OSB
108

O king of might and splendour,
creator most adored,
this sacrifice we render
to thee as sov'reign Lord.
May these our gifts be pleasing
unto thy majesty,
mankind from sin releasing
who have offended thee.

2
Thy body thou hast given,
thy blood thou hast outpoured,
that sin might be forgiven,
O Jesus, loving Lord.
As now with love most tender,
thy death we celebrate,
our lives in self-surrender
to thee we consecrate.

O little town of Bethlehem
Phillips Brooks (1835-93)
109

O little town of Bethlehem,
how still we see thee lie!
Above thy deep and dreamless sleep
the silent stars go by.
Yet, in thy dark streets shineth
the everlasting light;

the hopes and fears of all the years
are met in thee tonight.

2
O morning stars, together
proclaim the holy birth,
and praises sing to God the King,
and peace to men on earth;
for Christ is born of Mary;
and, gathered all above,
while mortals sleep, the angels keep
their watch of wondering love.

3
How silently, how silently,
the wondrous gift is given!
So God imparts to human hearts
the blessings of his heaven.
No ear may hear his coming;
but in this world of sin,
where meek souls will receive him, still
the dear Christ enters in.

4
O holy child of Bethlehem
descend to us we pray;
cast out our sin, and enter in,
be born in us to-day.
We hear the christmas angels
the great glad tidings tell:
O come to us, abide with us,
our Lord Émmanuel.

O Mary of graces
J. Rafferty
110

O Mary of graces and mother of Christ.
O may you direct me and guide me aright.
O may you protect me from Satan's control,
and may you protect me in body and soul.

2
O may you protect me by land and by sea,
and may you protect me from sorrows to be;
a strong guard of angels above me provide;
may God be before me and God at my side.

Once in royal David's city
Cecil Frances Alexander (1818-95)
111

Once in royal David's city
stood a lowly cattle shed,
where a mother laid her baby
in a manger for his bed;
Mary was that mother mild,
Jesus Christ her little child.

2
He came down to earth from heaven,
who is God and Lord of all,
and his shelter was a stable
and his cradle was a stall;
with the poor, oppressed, and lowly,
lived on earth our Saviour holy.

3
And through all his wondrous childhood
he would honour and obey,
love, and watch the lowly maiden
in whose gentle arms he lay;
Christian children, all must be
mild, obedient, good as he.

4
For he is our childhood's pattern,
day by day like us he grew;
he was little, weak and helpless,
tears and smiles like us he knew;
and he feeleth for our sadness,
and he shareth in our gladness.

5
And our eyes at last shall see him
through his own redeeming love,
for that child so dear and gentle
is our Lord in heaven above;
and he leads his people on
to the place where he is gone.

6
Not in that poor lowly stable,
with the oxen standing by,
we shall see him; but in heaven,
set at God's right hand on high;
when like stars his children crowned
all in white shall wait around.

O Sacred Head surrounded
112

13th century
tr. H. W. Baker—M. Farrell

O sacred head surrounded
by crown of piercing thorn.
O bleeding head so wounded,
reviled and put to scorn.
Our sins have marred the glory
of thy most holy face.
Yet angel hosts adore thee,
and tremble as they gaze.
2
The Lord of every nation
was hung upon a tree;
his death was our salvation,
our sins, his agony.
O Jesus, by thy Passion,
thy life in us increase;
thy death for us did fashion
our pardon and our peace.

O praise ye the Lord!
113

Henry Williams Baker (1821-77)
based on Psalms 148 and 150

O praise ye the Lord!
praise him in the height;
rejoice in his word,
ye angels of light;
ye heavens, adore him,
by whom ye were made,
and worship before him,
in brightness arrayed.
2
O praise ye the Lord!
praise him upon earth,
in tuneful accord,
ye sons of new birth.
Praise him who hath brought you
his grace from above,
praise him who hath taught you
to sing of his love.
3
O praise ye the Lord!
all things that give sound;
each jubilant chord
re-echo around;
loud organs, his glory
forth tell in deep tone,
and, sweet harp, the story
of what he hath done.
4
O praise ye the Lord!
thanksgiving and song
to him be outpoured
all ages along;
for love in creation,
for heaven restored,
for grace of salvation,
O praise ye the Lord!

O thou who at thy Eucharist didst pray
114

(from Jn 17) W.H. Turton

O thou who at thy Eucharist didst pray
that all the Church might be forever one.
Grant us at every eucharist to say
with longing heart and soul 'thy will be
done'.
O may we all one bread, one body be,
One through this sacrament of unity.
2
For all thy Church, O Lord, we intercede;
Make thou our sad divisions soon to cease;
Draw us the nearer each to each, we plead.
By drawing all to thee, O prince of peace;
Thus may we all one bread, one body be,
One through this sacrament of unity.
3
We pray thee too for wanderers from thy fold;
O bring them back, good shepherd of the sheep,
Back to the faith which saints believed of old,
Back to the Church which still that faith does
keep;
Soon may we all one bread, one body be.
One through this sacrament of unity.
4
So, Lord, at length when sacraments shall cease,
May we be one with all the Church above,
One with thy saints in one unbroken peace.
One with thy saints in one unbounded love:
More blessed still, in peace and love to be
One with the Trinity in unity

Pange lingua
St Thomas Aquinas (1227-74) **115**

Pange lingua gloriosi,
Corporis Mysterium,
Sanguinisque pretiosi
quem in mundi pretium,
fructus ventris generosi
Rex effudit gentium.
2
Nobis datus, nobis natus
ex intacta Virgine;
et in mundo conversatus,
sparso verbi semine,
sui moras incolatus
miro clausit ordine.
3
In supremae nocte coenae
recumbens cum fratribus,
observata lege plene
cibis in legalibus:
cibum turbae duodenae
se dat suis manibus.
4
Verbum caro, panem verum
Verbo carnem efficit:
fitque sanguis Christi merum;
et si sensus deficit,
ad firmandum cor sincerum
sola fides sufficit.
5
Tantum ergo Sacramentum
veneremur cernui;
et antiquum documentum
novo cedat ritui:
praestet fides supplementum
sensuum defectui.
6
Genitori, genitoque
laus, et jubilatio,
salus, honor, virtus quoque
sit et benedictio:
procedenti ab utroque
compar sit laudatio. Amen.

Praise the Lord
Lucien Deiss **116**

Alleluia, Amen!
Praise the Lord, all the peoples of the world!
Let all the nations give him honour!
2
His mercy for us has never failed;
the Lord remains true to his promise.
3
Praise the Father, the Son and Holy Spirit,
the God who is, for ages unending.

Alternative refrain (for use during Lent):
Glory to the Lord, Amen.

Praised be Christ's immortal body
St. Thomas Aguines (1227-74)
tr. M. Farrell **117**

Praised be Christ's immortal body,
and his precious blood be praised.
Born of royal virgin mother,
he shall reign for endless days.
Dying once to save all nations,
ever more he wins our praise.
2
Coming from the spotless virgin,
he for us was born a man.
Sowing seeds of truth among us,
he fulfilled the Father's plan.
Then his final night upon him,
wondrously that night began.
3
By a word, the Word among us
changes common bread and wine.
Bread becomes his holy body,
wine is made his blood divine.
Though his truth evades the senses,
faith unveils the sacred sign.
4
Humbly let us sing our homage
for so great a sacrament.

Let all former rites surrender
to the Lord's new testament.
What our senses fail to fathom
let us grasp through faith's consent.
5
Glory, honour, adoration,
let us sing with one accord.
praised be God, almighty Father,
praised be Christ his Son, our Lord.
Praised be God the Holy Spirit,
blessed Trinity adored.

Praise my soul the King of heaven
Henry Francis Lyte (1793-1847) **118**

Praise my soul the King of heaven,
to his feet your tribute bring.
Ransomed, healed, restored, forgiven,
who am I his praise to sing?
Praise him! Praise him! (2)
Praise the everlasting King!
2
Praise him for his grace and favour
to our fathers in distress;
praise him still the same for ever,
slow to chide and swift to bless.
Praise him! Praise him! (2)
Glorious in his faithfulness!
3
Fatherlike, he tends and spares us;
well our feeble frame he knows;
in his hands he gently bears us,
rescues us from all our foes.
Praise him! Praise him! (2)
Widely as his mercy flows!
4
Angels, help us to adore him;
you behold him face to face;
sun and moon bow down before him,
ev'ry thing in time and space.
Praise him! Praise him! (2)
Praise with us the God of grace!

Praise to the Lord

119

Praise to the Lord, the Almighty,
the King of creation!
O my soul, praise him,
for he is your health and salvation.
All you who hear,
now to his altar draw near,
join in profound adoration.

2
Praise to the Lord, let us offer
our gifts at his altar;
let not our sins and transgressions
now cause us to falter.
Christ, the High Priest,
bids us all join in his feast.
Victims with him on the altar.

3
Praise to the Lord, who will prosper our work
and defend us:
Surely his goodness and mercy here daily
attend us:
Ponder anew all the Almighty can do,
He who with love will befriend us.

4
Praise to the Lord, oh let all that is in us
adore him!
All that has life and breath, come now in
praises before him.
Let the Amen sound from his people again,
Now as we worship before him.

Priestly people
Lucien Deiss

120

Priestly people, Kingly people,
Holy people,
God's chosen people, sing praise to
the Lord.

We sing to you, O Christ, beloved Son
of the Father.
We give you praise, O Wisdom everlasting
and Word of God.

2
We sing to you, O Son born of Mary
the Virgin.
We give you praise, our brother born
to heal us, our saving Lord.

3
We sing to you, O brightness of splendour
and glory.
We give you praise, O morning star
announcing the coming day.

4
We sing to you, O light bringing men
out of darkness.
We give you praise, O guiding light
who shows us the way to heav'n.

5
We sing to you, Messiah foretold
by the prophets.
We give you praise, O Son of David
and Son of Abraham.

6
We sing to you, Messiah, the hope
of the people.
We give you praise, O Christ, our Lord
and King, humble, meek of heart.

7
We sing to you, the Way to the Father
in heaven.
We give you praise, the Way of Truth
and Way of all grace and light.

8
We sing to you, O Priest of the new
dispensation.
We give you praise, Our Peace,
sealed by the blood of the Sacrifice.

9
We sing to you, O Lamb, put to death
for sinners.
We give you praise, O Victim,
immolated for all mankind.

10
We sing to you, the Tabernacle
made by the Father.
We give you praise, the Cornerstone
and Saviour of Israel.

11
We sing to you, the Shepherd who leads
to the kingdom.
We give you praise, who gather
all your sheep in the one true fold.

12
We sing to you, O Fount, overflowing
with mercy.
We give you praise, who give us
living waters to quench our thirst.

13
We sing to you, True Vine, planted by God
our Father.
We give you praise, O blessed Vine,
whose branches bear fruit in love.

14
We sing to you, O Manna, which God gives
his people.
We give you praise, O living Bread,
which comes down to us from heaven.

15
We sing to you, the Image of Father
eternal.
We give you praise, O King of justice,
Lord, and the King of peace.

16
We sing to you, the First-born
of all God's creation.
We give you praise, Salvation of your saints
sleeping in the Lord.

17
We sing to you, O Lord, whom the Father
exalted.
We give you praise, in glory you are coming
to judge all men.

Praise to the Holiest
John Henry Newman (1801-90)

121

Praise to the Holiest in the height,
and in the depth be praise,
in all his words most wonderful,
most sure in all his ways.
2
O loving wisdom of our God!
When all was sin and shame,
a second Adam to the fight,
and to the rescue came.
3
O wisest love! that flesh and blood
which did in Adam fail,
should strive afresh against the foe,
should strive and should prevail.
4
And that a higher gift than grace
should flesh and blood refine,
God's presence and his very self,
and Essence all divine.
5
O generous love! that he who smote
in man for man the foe,
the double agony in man
for man should undergo.
6
And in the garden secretly
and on the cross on high,
should teach his brethren, and inspire
to suffer and to die.
7
Praise to the Holiest in the height,
and in the depth be praise,
in all his words most wonderful,
most sure in all his ways.

Praise God, from whom all blessings flow
Thomas Ken (1637-1710)

122

Praise God from whom all blessings flow,
praise him, all creatures here below.
Praise him above, ye heavenly host.
Praise Father, Son and Holy Ghost.

Regina caeli
Traditional anthem

123

Regina caeli, laetare, alleluia.
Quia quem meruisti portare, alleluia.
Resurrexit sicut dixit, alleluia.
Ora pro nobis Deum, alleluia.

Remember those, O Lord

124

Remember those, O Lord,
Who in your peace have died,
Yet may not gain love's high reward
Till love is purified!
2
With you they faced death's night,
Sealed with your victory sign,
Soon may the splendour of your light
On them for ever shine!
3
Sweet is their pain, yet deep,
Till perfect love is born;
Their lone night-watch they gladly keep
Before your radiant morn!
4
Your love is their great joy;
Your will their one desire;
As finest gold without alloy
Refine them in love's fire!
5
For them we humbly pray:
Perfect them in your love!
O may we share eternal day
With them in heaven above!

Receive O Father

125

Receive O Father in thy love,
These humble gifts of bread and wine.
That with ourselves we offer thee,
Returning gifts already thine.
2
Behold this host and chalice, Lord,
To thee on high the gifts we raise;
Through them may we our honour pay,
Our adoration and our praise.
3
No earthly claim to grace is ours,
Save what thy sacrifice has won;
Grant then thy grace, fulfil our needs,
And may thy will in ours be done.

Rorate caeli

126

*Rorate caeli desuper,
et nubes pluant justum.*
Ne irascaris Domine, ne ultra memineris
iniquitatis;
ecce civitas Sancti facta est deserta.
Sion deserta facta est, Jerusalem desolata est,
domus sanctificationis tuae et gloriae tuae,
ubi laudaverunt te patres nostri.
2
Peccavimus, et facti sumus tamquam immundus
nos,
et cecidimus quasi folium universi;
et iniquitates nostrae quasi ventus abstulerunt
nos,
abscondisti faciem tuam a nobis,
et allisisti nos in manu iniquitatis nostrae.
3
Vide Domine afflictionem populi tui,
et mitte quem missurus es;
emitte Agnum dominatorem terrae,
de petra deserti ad montem filiae Sion,
ut auferat ipse jugum captivitatis nostrae.

Salve Regina
Traditional anthem

Salve Regina, Mater misericordiae:
vita dulcedo, et spes nostra, salve.
Ad te clamamus, exules filii Hevae.
Ad te suspiramus, gementes et flentes,
in hac lacrimarum vale.

Eja ergo, Advocata nostra,
illos tuos misericordes oculos
ad nos converte.

Et Jesum benedictum fructum ventris tui
nobis post hoc exsilium ostende.
O clemens, O pia, O dulcis Virgo Maria.

Sancti venite
St Secundinus

Sancti venite, Corpus Christi sumite,
Sanctum bibentes, quo redempti, sanguinem,
2
Salvati Christi corpore et sanguine,
A quo refecti, laudes dicamus Deo.
3
Hoc Sacramento corporis et sanguinis,
Omnes exuti ab infernis faucibus.
4
Pro universis, immolatus Dominus,
Ipse sacerdos, existit et hostia.
5
Accedant omnes, pura mente creduli,
Sumant aeternam salutis custodiam.
6
Alpha et omega, ipse Christus Dominus,
Venit venturus, judicare homines.

Show us, Lord, the path of life
Psalm 15

Show us, Lord, the path of life.
Preserve me, God, I take refuge in you.
I say to the Lord "You are my God."
O Lord, it is you who are my portion and cup,
it is you yourself who are my prize.
2
I will bless the Lord who gives me counsel,
who even at night directs my heart.
I keep the Lord ever in my sight,
since he is at my right hand, I shall stand firm.
3
And so my heart rejoices, my soul is glad,
even my body shall rest in safety;
for you will not leave my soul among the dead,
nor let your beloved know decay.
4
You will show me the path of life,
the fullness of joy in your presence,
at your right hand, happiness for ever.

See amid the winter's snow
Edward Caswall (1814-78)

See, amid the winter's snow,
born for us on earth below,
see, the tender Lamb appears,
promised from eternal years.

Hail, thou ever-blessed morn,
hail, redemption's happy dawn!
Sing through all Jerusalem,
Christ is born in Bethlehem.

2
Lo, within a manger lies
he who built the starry skies;
he who, throned in heights sublime,
sits amid the cherubim.
3
Say, ye holy shepherds, say,
what your joyful news today?
Wherefore have ye left your sheep
on the lonely mountain steep?
4
'As we watched at dead of night,
lo, we saw a wondrous light;
angels, singing peace on earth,
told us of the Saviour's birth.'
5
Sacred infant, all divine,
what a tender love was thine,
thus to come from highest bliss,
down to such a world as this!
6
Virgin mother, Mary blest,
by the joys that fill thy breast,
pray for us, that we may prove
worthy of the Saviour's love.

'Sé an Tiarna m'aoire 131
Salm 22 (Fiontán P. ÓCearbhaill)

'Sé an Tiarna m'aoire;
ní bheidh aon ní de dhíth orm.

'Sé an Tiarna m'aoire;
ní bheidh aon ní de dhíth orm.
Cuireann sé 'mo luí mé
i móinéar féarghlas,
seolann sé ar imeall an uisce mé,
mar a bhfaighim suaimhneas.
2
Seolann sé mé ar rianta díreacha
mar gheall ar a ainm.
Fiú dá siúlfainn i ngleann an dorchadais,
níor bhaol liom an t-olc;
agus tú faram le do shlat is do bhachall,
chun sólás a thabhairt dom.
3
Cóiríonn tú bórd chun béile dom
i bhfianaise mo naimhde;
ungann tú mo cheann le hola;
tá mo chupán ag cur thar mhaoil.
4
Leanfaidh cineáltas is fábhar mé
gach uile lá de mo shaol;
i dteach an Tiarna a mhairfidh mé
go brách na breithe.

See how the rose of Judah 132
Es ist ein Ros—I. Udulutsch

See how the rose of Judah from tender
branch has sprung,
A rose from root of Jesse, as prophets
long had sung.
We sing that hymn again:
To God on high be glory,
and peace on earth to men.
2
This rose of royal beauty of which Isaiah sings,
Is Mary, maiden mother, and Christ the
flower she brings.
By God's unique design,
Remaining still a virgin, she bore a child divine.
3
We pray thee, Virgin Mother, the Queen
of heaven and earth:
Obtain for us from Jesus the blessings of
his birth.
By his humility.
May we live as God's children in peace and
unity.

See us, Lord, about thine altar 133
John Greally

See us, Lord, about thine altar;
though so many, we are one;
many souls by love united
in the heart of Christ thy Son.
2
Hear our prayers, O loving Father,
hear in them thy Son, our Lord;
hear him speak our love and worship,
as we sing with one accord.
3
Once were seen the blood and water;
now he seems but bread and wine;
then in human form he suffered,
now his form is but a sign.

4
Wheat and grape contain the meaning;
food and drink he is to all;
one in him, we kneel adoring,
gathered by his loving call.
5
Hear us yet; so much is needful
in our frail, disordered life;
stay with us and tend our weakness
till that day of no more strife.
6
Members of his mystic body
now we know our prayer is heard,
heard by thee, because thy children,
have received th'eternal Word.

Silent night 134
Joseph Mohr (1792-1848)
tr. J. Young

Silent night, holy night,
All is calm, all is bright,
round yon virgin mother and child;
holy infant so tender and mild;
sleep in heavenly peace. (2)
2
Silent night, holy night,
Shepherds quake at the sight,
glories stream from heaven afar,
heavenly hosts sing alleluia:
Christ, the Saviour is born. (2)
3
Silent night, holy night,
Son of God, love's pure light,
radiant beams from thy holy face,
with the dawn of redeeming grace:
Jesus, Lord, at thy birth. (2)

Show us, Lord, your mercy
Psalm 84

135

Show us, Lord, your mercy
And grant us your salvation.

I will hear what the Lord has to say,
a voice that speaks of peace,
peace for his people and his friends.
His help is near for those who fear him
and his glory will dwell in our land.
2
Mercy and faithfulness have met,
justice and peace have embraced.
Faithfulness shall spring from the earth
and justice look down from heaven.
3
The Lord will make us prosper
and our earth shall yield its fruit.
Justice shall march before him
and peace shall follow his steps.

Sing praise to our Creator
M. Evans

136

Sing praise to our Creator,
O sons of Adam's race,
God's children by adoption,
baptised into his grace.
Praise the holy Trinity,
undivided unity;
Holy God, mighty God,
God immortal, be adored.
2
To Jesus Christ give glory,
God's co-eternal Son;
as members of his body,
we live in him as one.
Praise the holy Trinity,
undivided unity,
Holy God, mighty God,
God immortal, be adored.

3
Now praise the Holy Spirit
poured forth upon the earth;
who sanctifies and guides us,
confirmed in our rebirth.
Praise the holy Trinity,
undivided unity.
Holy God, mighty God,
God immortal, be adored.

Sing praise to the Lord
all our days
John V. Moloney
(based on Psalm 102)

137

Sing praise to the Lord all our days.
God's chosen people now bless his
holy name.

Forgiving our offences,
he crowns us with his love.
From every depth he lifts us,
to share his life above.
2
As far as earth from heaven,
as far as east from west,
he puts our sins behind him,
he comforts the oppressed.
3
The Lord is slow to anger,
compassionate and kind,
with tender love he guards us,
as father treats his child.

Sing to the Lord, Alleluia
John Foley SJ, from Psalm 95

138

Sing to the Lord, Alleluia,
Sing to the Lord.

Bless his name;
Announce his salvation
day after day.
Alleluia.
2
Give to him
You fam'lies of peoples,
glory and praise.
Alleluia.
3
Great is he
And worthy of praises,
day after day.
Alleluia.
4
He it is
Who gave us the heavens.
Glory to God.
Alleluia.
5
Tell his glories,
Tell all the nations
day after day.
Alleluia.
6
Bring your gifts
And enter his temple;
Worship the Lord.
Alleluia.

Síormholadh is glóir duit

139

Tadhg Ó Sé

Síormholadh is glóir duit, a Athair shíoraí,
A gheall dúinn an tsíocháin leat féin i do
ríocht.
Is d'Aon Mhac nuair d'fhuascail Síol Éabh, lena
bhás,
Gur réitigh an ród dúinn chun aontacht is páirt
Ón gcroí gabhaimid buíochas
As ucht an tsoiscéil sin,
'S é Pádraig a chraol é fá ghríosadh an ghrá.

An ghlóir atá 'ndán dúinn id briathar is léir
'T'réis m'ardú ón talamh 'sé ardóidh mé gach
aon'
Go raibh muid, a Dhia dhil, 'nar scáthán go deo
Díot féin le grá's páirt, as nós Pádraig fadó.
Aon anró níor brí leis
Ach briathar Dé 'chraoladh
Is míorúilt grá Dé 'dhéanamh 'n uile rud nua.

Soul of my Saviour

140

*Ascribed to John XXII
(1249-1334), tr. Anonymous*

Soul of my Saviour, sanctify my breast;
Body of Christ, be thou my saving guest;
Blood of my Saviour, bathe me in thy tide,
wash me ye waters streaming from his side.

Strength and protection may thy Passion be;
O Blessed Jesus, hear and answer me;
deep in thy wounds, Lord, hide and
shelter me;
so shall I never, never part from thee.

3
Guard and defend me from the foe malign;
in death's dread moments make me
only thine;
call me, and bid me come to thee on high,
when I may praise thee with thy
saints for aye.

Stabat mater dolorosa

141

Jacopone da Todi (d. 1306)

Stabat mater dolorósa
juxta crucem lacrymósa
dum pendébat Fílius.
2
Cujus ánimam geméntem
contristátam et doléntem,
pertransívit gládius.
3
O quam tristis, et afflícta,
fuit illa benedícta
Mater Unigéniti!
4
Quae moerébat, et dolébat,
Pía Mater, dum vidébat
nati poenas ínclyti.
5
Quis est homo, qui non fleret,
Matrem Christi si vidéret
in tanto supplício?
6
Quis non posset contristári,
Christi matrem contemplári,
doléntem cum Fílio?
7
Pro peccátis suae gentis,
vidit Jesum in torméntis
et flagéllis súbditum.
8
Vidit suum dulcem Natum
moriéndo desolátum,
dum emísit spíritum.
9
Eja, Mater, fons amóris,
me sentíre vim dolóris
fac, ut tecum lúgeam.
10
Fac, ut árdeat cor meum
in amándo Christum Deum,
ut sibi compláceam.

11
Sancta Mater, istud agas
Crucifíxi fige plagas
cordi meo válide.
12
Tui nati vulneráti,
tam dignáti pro me pati,
poenas mecum dívide.
13
Fac me tecum pie flere,
Crucifíxo condolére,
donec ego víxero.
14
Juxta crucem tecum stare,
et me tibi sociáre
in planctu desídero
15
Quando corpus moriétur,
fac ut ánimae donétur
Paradísi glória. Amen.

Stay with us, Lord, we pray you

142

John V. Moloney

Stay with us, Lord, we pray you, alleluia.

You are the bread come down from heaven;
you are the food of life eternal,
2
You are the light which illumines the world,
brightening our way, dispelling
our darkness.
3
You are the Christ, the divine Son of God,
you are the pledge of life eternal.

Star of sea and ocean
Ralph Wright

143

Star of sea and ocean,
gateway to man's heaven,
mother of our Maker,
hear our pray'r, O Maiden.
2
Welcoming the *Ave*
of God's simple greeting,
you have borne a Saviour
far beyond all dreaming.
3
Loose the bonds that hold us
bound in sin's own blindness,
that with eyes now open'd
God's own light may guide us.
4
Show yourself our mother,
he will hear your pleading,
whom your womb has sheltered
and whose hand brings healing.
5
Gentlest of all virgins,
that our love be faithful,
keep us from all evil
gentle, strong and grateful.
6
Guard us through life's dangers,
never turn and leave us,
may our hope find harbour
in the calm of Jesus.
7
Sing to God our Father
through the Son who saves us,
joyful in the Spirit,
everlasting praises.

Sweet sacrament divine
Francis Stanfield (1835-1914)
and Donal Murray

144

Sweet sacrament divine,
our shepherd and our King,
around your earthly shrine,
with grateful hearts we sing;
Jesus, to you our voice we raise,
in songs of love and joyful praise,
sweet sacrament divine. (2)
2
Sweet sacrament of peace,
in you mankind is blessed.
All pain and sorrows cease
and human hearts find rest.
Upon your promise we rely:
"Who eats this bread will never die."
Sweet sacrament of peace. (2)

Tantum Ergo
St Thomas Aquinas (1227-74)

145

Tantum ergo Sacramentum
veneremur cernui:
et antiquum documentum
novo cedat ritui;
praestet fides supplementum
sensuum defectui.
2
Genitori, genitoque
laus et jubilatio,
salus, honor, virtus quoque
sit et benedictio;
procedenti ab utroque
compar sit laudatio. Amen.

The bells of the angelus
Author unknown

146

The bells of the angelus
call us to pray;
in sweet tones announcing
the sacred Ave.
Ave, ave, ave, Maria:
Ave, ave, ave, Maria.
2
An angel of mercy
led Bernadette's feet
where flows the deep torrent
Our Lady to greet.
3
She prayed to our mother
that God's will be done:
she prayed for his glory
that his kingdom come.
4
Immaculate Mary,
your praises we sing
who reign now with Christ,
our redeemer and king.
5
In heaven the blessed
your glory proclaim,
on earth now your children
invoke your fair name.

The Church's one foundation
S.J. Stone (1830-1900)

147

The Church's one foundation,
is Jesus Christ, her Lord;
she is his new creation,
by water and the Word;
from heav'n he came and sought her
to be his holy bride,
with his own blood he bought her,
and for her life he died.
2
Elect from every nation,
yet one o'er all the earth,
her charter of salvation,
one Lord, one faith, one birth;
one holy name she blesses,
partakes one holy food,
and to one hope she presses,
with every grace embued.
3
'Mid toil, and tribulation,
and tumult of her war,
she waits the consummation
of peace for evermore;
till with the vision glorious
her longing eyes are blest,
and the great Church victorious
shall be the Church at rest.
4
Yet she on earth hath union
with God the Three in One,
and mystic sweet communion
with those whose rest is won:
O happy ones and holy!
Lord, give us grace that we
like them, the meek and lowly
on high may dwell with thee.

The light of Christ
Donald Fishel

148

*The light of Christ
has come into the world. (Repeat)*

All men must be born again
to see the kingdom of God;
the water and the Spirit
bring new life in God's love.
2
God gave up his only Son
out of love for the world,
so that all men who believe in him
will live for ever.
3
The light of God has come to us
so that we might have salvation;
from the darkness of our sins we walk
into glory with Christ Jesus.

The day thou gavest
John Ellerton (1826-93)

149

The day thou gavest, Lord, is ended:
the darkness falls at thy behest;
to thee our morning hymns ascended;
thy praise shall sanctify our rest.
2
We thank thee that thy Church unsleeping,
while earth rolls onward into light,
through all the world her watch is keeping,
and rests not now by day or night.
3
As o'er each continent and island
the dawn leads on another day,
the voice of prayer is never silent,
nor dies the strain of praise away.
4
The sun that bids us rest is waking
our brethren 'neath the western sky,
and hour by hour fresh lips are making
thy wondrous doings heard on high.

5
So be it, Lord; thy throne shall never,
like earth's proud empire, pass away;
thy kingdom stands, and grows for ever,
till all thy creatures own thy sway.

The King of love, my shepherd is

150

The King of love, my shepherd is,
Whose goodness fails me, never;
I nothing lack if I am his,
And he is mine for ever.
2
Where streams of living waters flow,
To rest my soul he leads me;
Where fresh and fertile pastures grow,
With heav'nly food he feeds me.
3
Perverse and foolish I have strayed,
But he with love has sought me,
And on his shoulder gently laid,
And home, rejoicing, brought me.
4
In death's dark vale I fear no ill,
With you, dear Lord, beside me;
Your rod and staff my comfort still,
Your cross will ever guide me.
5
You spread a banquet in my sight,
My head with oil anointing,
And let me taste the sweet delight,
From your pure chalice flowing.
6
And so through all my length of days,
Your goodness fails me never;
Good shepherd, may I sing your praise,
Within your house for ever.

The first Nowell
Traditional Old English

151

The first Nowell the angel did say
was to certain poor shepherds in
fields as they lay:
in fields where they lay keeping their sheep,
on a cold winter's night that was so deep.
Nowell, Nowell, Nowell, Nowell,
born is the King of Israel!

2
They lookéd up and saw a star.
Shining in the east, beyond them far,
And to the earth it gave great light,
And so it continued both day and night.

3
And by the light of that same star,
Three wise men came from country far,
To seek for a king was their intent,
And to follow the star wherever it went.

4
This star drew nigh to the north-west,
O'er Bethlehem it took its rest.
And there it did both stop and stay,
Right over the place where Jesus lay.

5
Then did they know assuredly
Within that house the King did lie:
They entered in then for to see,
And found the babe in poverty.

6
Then entered in those wise men three,
Full reverently upon their knee.
And offered there in his presence
Their gold and myrrh and frankincense.

7
Then let us all with one accord
Sing praises to our heavenly Lord.
That hath made heaven and earth of nought,
And with his blood mankind hath bought.

The Lord is my shepherd
Psalm 22 (Thomas Egan)

152

The Lord is my Shepherd,
there is nothing I shall want.

The Lord is my Shepherd.
There is nothing I shall want.
Fresh and green are the pastures
where he gives me repose.

2
Near restful waters he leads me,
to revive my drooping spirit.
He guides me along the right path.
He is true to his name.

3
If I should walk in the valley of darkness,
no evil would I fear.
You are there with your crook
and your staff,
with these you give me comfort.

4
You have prepared a banquet for me,
in the sight of my foes.
My head you have anointed with oil,
my cup is overflowing.

5
Surely his goodness and kindness
shall follow me,
all the days of my life.
In the Lord's own house shall I dwell,
for ever and ever.

The Lord's my shepherd
Paraphrased from Ps. 22(23)
in the "Scottish Psalter" (1650)

153

The Lord's my shepherd, I'll not want,
he makes me down to lie
in pastures green he leadeth me
the quiet waters by.

2
My soul he doth restore again,
and me to walk doth make
within the paths of righeousness,
e'en for his own name's sake.

3
Yea, though I walk in death's dark vale,
yet will I fear no ill,
For thou art with me, and thy rod
and staff me comfort still.

4
My table thou hast furnished
in presence of my foes,
my head thou dost with oil anoint,
and my cup overflows.

5
Goodness and mercy all my life
shall surely follow me.
And in God's house for evermore
my dwelling-place shall be.

The Lord Jesus
Gregory Norbert, O.S.B.

154

The Lord Jesus, after
eating with his friends,
washed their feet and said to them:
'Do you know what I, your Lord, have done
to you?
I have given you example, that so you also
should do'.

You are my friends, a man can have no
greater love
than to give his life for his friends.

2
Peace I leave with you, my peace I give to all
who live with boundless love for humankind.

3
I am the vine and you the branch, remain
in me and you will bear abundant fruit.

4
Those who come to me will never thirst,
nor want for food and I will raise them up
on the last day.

The Lord made known to Israel
Donal Murray

155

The Lord made known to Israel
his great redeeming plan.
He speaks to us his people now,
through Christ his Son made man.
We have been called like Israel
to witness to God's grace,
a people he has made his own,
a royal priestly race.
2
God brought his people to the mount,
as we are gathered now,
to hear his holy word proclaimed
and their allegiance vow.
We have been called like Israel
to witness to God's grace,
a people he has made his own,
a royal priestly race.

Therefore, we before him bending

156

Therefore we before him bending
This great sacrament revere
Types and shadows have their ending,
For the perfect rite is here.
Faith, our outward sense befriending,
Makes the inward vision clear.
2
Glory, let us give, and blessing.
To the Father and the Son:
Honour, might and praise addressing,
While eternal ages run.
Ever too his love confessing.
Who, from both, with both is one.

The seed is Christ's
Words translated by James Quinn

157

The seed is Christ's, the harvest his;
may we be stored within God's barn.
The sea is Christ's, the fish are his:
may we be caught within God's net.
From birth to age, from age to death,
enfold us, Christ, within your arms.
Until the end, the great re-birth,
Christ, be our joy in Paradise.

This day God gives me
*James Quinn, S.J. (adapted from
'St. Patrick's Breastplate'. 8th cent)*

158

This day God gives me
strength of high heaven,
sun and moon shining,
flame in my hearth,
flashing of lightning,
wind in its swiftness,
deeps of the ocean,
firmness of earth.
2
This day God sends me
strength as my steersman,
might to uphold me,
wisdom as guide.
Your eyes are watchful,
your ears are listening,
your lips are speaking,
friend at my side.
3
God's way is my way,
God's shield is round me,
God's host defends me,
saving from ill.
Angels of heaven,
drive from me always
all that would harm me,
stand by me still.

4
Rising, I thank you,
mighty and strong one,
king of creation,
giver of rest,
firmly confessing
threeness of persons,
oneness of Godhead,
Trinity blest.

This is my will
James Quinn, S.J.

159

This is my will, my one command,
that love should dwell among you all.
This is my will that you should love
as I have shown that I love you.
2
No greater love a man can have
than that he die to save his friends.
You are my friends if you obey
What I command that you should do.
3
I call you now no longer slaves;
no slave knows all his master does.
I call you friends, for all I hear
my Father say, you hear from me.
4
You chose not me, but I chose you,
that you should go and bear much fruit.
I chose you out that you in me
should bear much fruit that will abide.
5
All that you ask my Father dear
for my name's sake you shall receive.
This is my will, my one command,
that love should dwell in each, in all.

160
To Christ, the Prince of Peace
E. Caswell

To Christ, the Prince of Peace,
And Son of God, most high.
The Father of the world to come,
Sing we with holy joy.
2
Take us to thy dear heart.
For there we long to be.
To find thy grace, and after death
Thine immortality.
3
Praise to the Father be,
And sole-begotten Son:
Praise holy Paraclete, to thee.
While endless ages run.

161
To Jesus Christ our sov'reign King
M.B. Hellriegel

To Jesus Christ our sov'reign King,
who is the world's Salvation.
All praise and homage do we bring
and thanks and adoration.
Christ Jesus Victor, Christ Jesus Ruler.
Christ Jesus, Lord and Redeemer.
2
Your reign extend, O King benign,
To ev'ry land and nation:
For in your kingdom Lord divine,
Alone we find salvation.
3
To you and to your Church, great King,
We pledge our hearts oblation.
Until before your throne we sing
In endless jubilation.

162
To thee, O Heart of Jesus

To thee, O Heart of Jesus,
to thee, our hearts we give.
Help, help us all to love thee,
and serve thee while we live.
Yes, yes, till life is over,
and then, for evermore,
O Sacred Heart of Jesus
we'll love thee and adore.
2
For us thy life of labour,
For us thy death of pain,
For us in guise so lowly,
Thou dost on earth remain.
3
No heart can be so tender,
No heart can love like thee,
Thy life-blood all, O Jesus,
was shed to set us free.

163
Veni Creator Spiritus
Attributed to Rabanus Maurus
(766-856)

Veni, Creator Spiritus,
mentes tuorum visita,
imple superna gratia,
quae tu creasti pectora.
2
Qui diceris Paraclitus,
Altissimi donum Dei,
fons vivus, ignis, caritas,
et spiritalis unctio.
3
Tu septiformis munere,
digitus paternae dexterae.
Tu rite promissum Patris,
sermone ditans guttura.

4
Accende lumen sensibus,
infunde amorem cordibus,
infirma nostri corporis
virtute firmans perpeti.
5
Hostem repellas longius,
pacemque dones protinus:
ductore sic te praevio,
vitemus omne noxium.
6
Per te sciamus, da, Patrem,
noscamus atque Filium,
teque utriusque Spiritum
credamus omni Tempore.
7
Deo Patri sit gloria,
et Filio, qui a mortuis
surrexit, ac Paraclito,
in saeculorum saecula. Amen.

164
Ubi Caritas

Ubi caritas est vera, Deus ibi est.

Congregavit nos in unum Christi amor.
Exsultemus et in ipso iucundemur.
Timeamus et amemus Deum vivum.
Et ex corde diligamus nos sincero.
2
Simul ergo cum in unum congregamur:
Ne nos mente dividamur, caveamus.
Cessent iurgia maligna, cessent lites.
Et in medio nostri sit Christus Deus.
3
Simul quoque cum beatis videamus
Glorianter vultum tuum, Christe Deus:
Gaudium, quod est immensum atque probum,
Saecula per infinita saeculorum.

We praise you and thank you — 165
Hymn to St Patrick –
Donal Murray

We praise you and thank you our Father above,
Who offer us peace in your Kingdom of love.
The world has been saved by the death of your
Son,
Who showed us the way that we all might be
one.
Accepting this Gospel we honour Saint Patrick,
Who taught in our land what your kindness
has done.
2
Your Word has revealed what our future will be,
'Raised up from the earth I draw people to me'.
May we like Saint Patrick bear witness to you,
Reflecting your love in whatever we do.
He came to our country which once had
enslaved him,
To preach the good news that God makes all
things new.

We three kings of orient are — 166
J.H. Hopkins (1822-1900)

We three kings of Orient are;
bearing gifts we traverse afar,
field and fountain, moor and mountain,
following yonder star.

O Star of wonder, star of night,
star with royal beauty bright,
westward leading, still proceeding,
guide us to thy perfect light.
2
Born a King on Bethlehem plain,
gold I bring, to crown him again,
King for ever, ceasing never,
over us all to reign.

3
Frankincense to offer have I,
incense owns a Deity nigh.
Prayer and praising, mankind raising,
worship him, God, most high.
4
Myrrh is mine, its bitter perfume
breathes a life of gathering gloom;
sorrowing, sighing, bleeding, dying,
sealed in the stone-cold tomb.
5
Glorious now behold him arise,
King and God and sacrifice;
Heav'n sings alleluia,
alleluia the earth replies.

We praise you God. (Te Deum) — 167
Ascribed to St Nicetas (c. 335)

We praise you, God, confessing you as Lord!
Eternal Father, all earth worships you!
Angelic choirs, high heavens, celestial powers,
Cherubs and seraphs praise you ceaselessly:
'All-holy Lord O God of heavenly hosts,
Your glorious majesty fills heaven and earth!'
2
Blessed apostles join in praise of you!
With prophets famed and martyrs clothed in
white,
Singing with Holy Church throughout the
earth:
'Father, we praise your boundless majesty!
We praise your glorious, true and only Son!
We praise you, Holy Spirit, Paraclete!"
3
You are the King of glory, Jesus Christ!
You are the Father's everlasting Son!
Born for mankind from lowly virgin's womb,
Death you have conquered, opening heaven
to faith!
Throned now in glory at the Father's side,
You shall return, faith teaches, as our judge!

4
We pray you, therefore, give your servants aid,
Whom you have ransomed with your precious
Blood!
Let them be ranked in glory with your saints!
Save, Lord, the people who are wholly yours!
Bless them, for they are your inheritance,
And, as their ruler, ever raise them up!
5
Throughout each single day we bless you,
Lord;
For all eternity we praise your name!
Keep us this day, Lord, free from every sin!
Have mercy on us, Lord; have mercy, Lord!
Show us your love, as we have hoped in you!
You are my hope, Lord! You shall fail me not!

V. Blessed are you, O Lord, O God of our
fathers.
R. You are worthy of praise and full of glory
for ever.
V. Let us give thanks to the Father, the Son
and the Holy Spirit.
R. Let us praise and exalt him for ever.
V. Blessed are you, O Lord, our God, in high
heaven.
R. You are worthy of praise and full of glory
for ever.

Let us pray.
There is no limit, O God, to your kindness,
nor can the riches of your bounty ever fail you.
We thank you for the gifts you have given us.
Prepare us for the good things in store for us
by showing us always your mercy. Through
Christ our Lord. Amen.

Whatsoever you do
Willard F. Jabusch

168

Whatsoever you do
to the least of my brothers,
that you do unto me.

When I was hungry
you gave me to eat.
When I was thirsty
you gave me to drink.
Now enter into the
home of my Father.
2
When I was homeless
you opened your door.
When I was naked
you gave me your coat.
Now enter into the
home of my Father.
3
When I was weary
you helped me find rest.
When I was anxious
you calmed all my fears.
Now enter into the
home of my Father.
4
When in a prison
you came to my cell.
When on a sick bed
you cared for my needs.
Now enter into the
home of my Father.
5
When I was aged
you bothered to smile.
When I was restless
you listened and cared.
Now enter into the
home of my Father.

6
When I was laughed at
you stood by my side.
When I was happy
you shared in my joy.
Now enter into the
home of my Father.

When I behold the wondrous Cross
I. Watts

169

When I behold the wondrous Cross,
on which the prince of glory died.
My richest gain I count but loss,
and pour contempt on all my pride.
2
Forbid it, Lord, that I should boast.
Save in the death of Christ, my God;
The vain things that attract me most,
I sacrifice them to his blood.
3
See, from his head, his hands, his feet,
What grief and love flow mingled down:
Did e'er such love and sorrow meet.
Or thorns compose so rich a crown?
4
Were all the realm of nature mine,
It would be offering far too small;
Love so amazing, so divine,
Demands my soul, my life, my all.

While shepherds watched
Nahum Tate (1652-1715)

170

While shepherds watched their flocks
by night,
all seated on the ground,
the Angel of the Lord came down,
and glory shone around.
2
'Fear not,' said he, (for mighty dread
had seized their troubled mind)
'Glad tidings of great joy I bring
to you and all mankind.'
3
'To you in David's town this day
is born of David's line,
a Saviour, who is Christ the Lord;
and this shall be the sign:'
4
'The heavenly Babe you there shall find
to human view displayed,
all meanly wrapped in swathing bands,
and in a manger laid.'
5
Thus spake the Seraph; and forthwith
appeared a shining throng
of Angels praising God, who thus
addressed their joyful song:
6
'All glory be to God on high,
and on the earth be peace,
goodwill henceforth from heaven to men
begin and never cease.'

Without seeing you
Lucien Deiss

171

Without seeing you, we love you.
Without seeing you, we believe.
And we sing, Lord, in joy, your glory.
You are our saviour,
We believe in you.

Blessed are they who will listen to your Word,
They shall truly never see death,
for by you, they are heirs to a new life.
O Lord, to whom shall we go?
You alone have the words of eternal life.
2
Those who live in the Spirit of the Word,
they shall find their true life in you,
and the truth of your Word makes them free,
Lord.
O Lord, to whom shall we go?
You alone have the words of eternal life.
3
By our faith you abide within our hearts,
keep us safely with you in love.
Give all people the hope of your power,
Lord.
O Lord, to whom shall we go?
You alone have the words of eternal life.
4
All my faith is in him who died for me,
for it is not I now who live.
It is Christ now in me, my salvation.
O Lord, to whom shall we go?
You alone have the words of eternal life.
5
By your grace you have saved us from our sins,
in our hearts you nourish our faith.
Our salvation is wrought by your mercy.
O Lord, to whom shall we go?
You alone have the words of eternal life.

6
In our hearts may the fire of love still burn.
Here you give your Spirit to us,
and the flame of that fire fills the whole world.
O Lord, to whom shall we go?
You alone have the words of eternal life.
7
May we live in the brightness of your joy.
May we know the peace of your love.
May we sing of your glory forever.
O Lord, to whom shall we go?
You alone have the words of eternal life.
8
Reunite all your people in one faith.
Lead us all to heavenly joy.
We will see your face for all ages.
O Lord, to whom shall we go?
You alone have the words of eternal life.

Yes, I shall arise
Lucien Deiss

172

Yes, I shall arise and return
to my Father

To you, O Lord, I lift up my soul,
In you, O my God, I place all my trust.
2
Look down on me, have mercy, O Lord.
Forgive me my sins, behold all my grief.
3
Do not withold your goodness from me,
O Lord, may your love be deep in my soul.
4
Mercy, I cry, O Lord, wash me clean.
And whiter than snow my spirit shall be.
5
Give me again the joy of your help.
Now open my lips, your praise I will sing.
6
My soul will sing, my heart will rejoice.
The blessings of God will fill all my days.

You are the honour
Lucien Deiss

173

You are the honour,
you are the glory of our people.
Holy Virgin Mary.

You are the glory of Jerusalem,
Holy Virgin Mary.
2
You are the greatest joy of Israel,
Holy Virgin Mary.
3
You are the highest honour of our race,
Holy Virgin Mary. *Repeat refrain.*
4
May you be blessed by the Lord most high,
Holy Virgin Mary.
5
Now and for all ages without end,
Holy Virgin Mary.
6
Give praise to God in the Church and Christ,
Holy Virgin Mary. *Repeat refrain.*

Ceol an Aifrinn
Seán Ó Riada

KYRIE ELEISON

A Thiarna, déan tró-caire. A Chríost, déan tró-caire. A Thiarna, déan tró-caire.

AN GHLÓIR

Glóir do Dhia sna har—da. Ag-us ar tha-lamh sío-cháin do lucht a

pháir—te. Molaimid Thú. Móraimid Thú. Adhraimid Thú. Tugaimid

glóir duit. Gabhaimid buíochas leat as ucht do mhór-ghlóir——e. A

Thiarna Dia, a Rí na bhFlaitheas, a Dhia, a Athair uile-chumhachtaigh. A

Thiarna aonmhic, Íosa Chríost. A Thiarna Dia, a Uain Dé, Mac an

Athar. Tusa a thógas peacaí an domhain, déan tró-cai-re 'rainn.

Tusa a thógas peacaí an domhain, glac le-nár

CEOL AN AIFRINN
Cóipcheart © Seán Ó Riada
An clóchur seo
le caoinchead:
An Clóchomhar Tta

174

174

CEOL AN AIFRINN
Cóipcheart © Seán Ó Riada
An clóchur seo
le caoinchead:
An Clóchomhar Tta

Tusa a—tá i do shuí ar dheis an Athar, déan tró-cai-re 'rainn. Óir is

Tú amháin is naofa. Is Tú amháin is Tiarna. Is Tú amháin is ró-

ard, a Íosa Críost, mar aon leis an Spiorad Naomh i nglóir Dé an

tAth air. A ——————— men.

SANCTUS

Is Naofa, Naofa, Naofa Tú, a Thiarna, Dia na

Slua. Tá neamh a-gus talamh lán de do ghlóir. Hó—sanna sna

har ——da. Is beannaithe 'n té 'tá ag teacht in ain-m an

Tiar——na. Hó—san-na sna har——da.

AN PHAIDIR

Ár nAthair a—tá ar neamh, go naofar tAinm, go dtaga do
ríocht, go ndéantar do thoil ar an dtalamh mar a ní — thear ar
neamh. Ár n-arán lae—thiúil tabhair dúinn in—niu, agus maith dúinn ár
bhfia—cha, mar mhaithimíd d'ár bhféi-chiúna féin. A's ná lig sinn i gcathú, ach saor sinn ó olc.

AGNUS DEI

A Uain Dé, a thógas peacaí an domhain, déan trócaire 'rainn. A
Uain Dé, a thógas peacaí an domhain, déan trócaire 'rainn. A
Uain Dé, a thógas peacaí an domhain, tabhair dúinn síc —cháin.

CEOL AN AIFRINN
Cóipcheart © Seán Ó Riada
An clóchur seo
le caoinchead:
An Clóchomhar Tta

174

A Mass for Peace

Thomas C Kelly

LORD HAVE MERCY

A MASS FOR PEACE
Copyright © Thomas C Kelly

175

Lord have mer - cy, Lord have mer - cy. Christ have mer - cy,
Christ have mer - cy. Lord have mer - cy. Lord have mer - cy, have mer - cy.

GLORIA

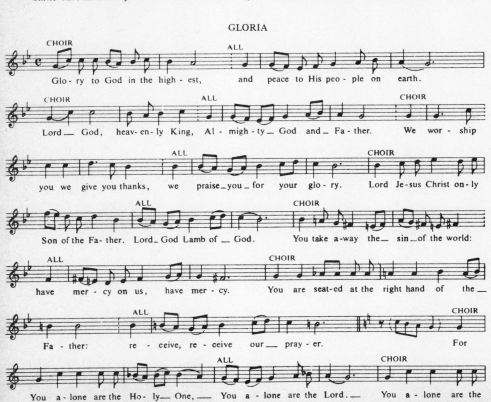

Glo - ry to God in the high - est, and peace to His peo - ple on earth.

Lord God, heav - en - ly King, Al - migh - ty God and Fa - ther. We wor - ship

you we give you thanks, we praise you for your glo - ry. Lord Je - sus Christ on - ly

Son of the Fa - ther. Lord God Lamb of God. You take a - way the sin of the world:

have mer - cy on us, have mer - cy. You are seat - ed at the right hand of the

Fa - ther: re - ceive, re - ceive our pray - er. For

You a - lone are the Ho - ly One, You a - lone are the Lord. You a - lone are the

175

A MASS FOR PEACE
Copyright © Thomas C Kelly

ALL · Most High, the Most High Je-sus Christ. CHOIR With the Ho-ly Spir-it in the glo-ry of God, in the glo-ry of God the Fa - ther A - men.

GOSPEL ACCLAMATION

Al-le-lu-ia. Al-le-lu-ia. Al - le-lu-ia.

HOLY, HOLY, HOLY

ALL Ho-ly, ho-ly, ho-ly Lord, God of pow'r and might. Heav'n and earth are full of Your glo-ry. Ho-san-na in the high-est. CHOIR Bless-ed is he who comes, in the name of the Lord. Ho-san-na, ho-san-na. Ho-san-na in the high-est.

MEMORIAL ACCLAMATION

Christ has died Christ is risen, Christ will come a-gain.

GREAT AMEN

A - men. A - men.

OUR FATHER

Our Fa-ther who art in heav'n. Hallowed be Thy Name. Thy King-dom come Thy will be done on earth as it is in heav'n. Give us this day our dai-ly bread and for-give us our tres-pass-es, as we for-give those who tres-pass a-gainst us, and lead us not in to temp-ta-tion, but de-liv-er us from ev-il.

ACCLAMATION

For the King-dom, the pow'r and the glo-ry are yours now and for-ev-er.

LAMB OF GOD

CHOIR Lamb of God, you take a-way the sins of the world: ALL have mer-cy on us.

CHOIR Lamb of God, you take a-way the sins of the world: ALL have mer-cy on us.

CHOIR Lamb of God, you take a-way the sins of the world: ALL Grant us peace.

THE IRISH EPISCOPAL COMMISSION FOR LITURGY   ADVISORY COMMITTEE ON CHURCH MUSIC

HOSANNA!

A NATIONAL LITURGICAL SONGBOOK FOR IRELAND
SUPPLEMENT 1 (Nos 176-199)

GENERAL EDITOR: PAUL KENNY

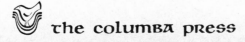 the columba press

the columba press

8 Lr Kilmacud Road,
Blackrock, Co Dublin.

First edition 1987
Designed by Bill Bolger
Typeset by Typeform, Dublin
Music setting by
Seton Music Graphics, Bantry.
Printed in Ireland by
Mount Salus Press, Dublin.

ISBN: 0 948183 46 2

Sole distributors in Northern Ireland:
DRC BOOKSHOPS
22/24 Fleetwood Street
Belfast BT14 6AX

The editor and the publishers thank the following for permission to use material in their copyright:

Fr Pat Ahern (No 194); Jacques Berthier/Collins Liturgical Publications, London (No 196); Shane Brennan (No 187); Co-operative Ministries Inc. Washington (Nos 179,188,191,198); Sr Margaret Daly, OCSO (No 189); Fr Tom Egan (No 185); GIA Publications Inc Chicago (Nos 180,199); David Haas (Nos 198,199); Marty Haugen (No 180); Michael Joncas (No 179); Magnificat Music, London (Nos 18 192); Fr Dermod McCarthy (No 194); Josephine O'Carroll (Nos 177,184); Ath Oilibhéar Ó Croiligh (No 194); Ite O'Donovan (Nos 178,183,197); Ath Diarmuid Ó'Laoghaire, SJ (No 197); Tadhg Ó Shéaghdha (No 184); Sr Aideen O'Sullivan (No 193); David Saint (No 190); John Scalea (No 191); Christopher Walker (Nos 176,186,195); A. P. Watt Ltd, London for Grail Psalms 24,95,116,117 and the Benedictus Canticle; International Committee on English in the Liturgy, Washington (Nos 181,183,18 190).

Compilation copyright © 1987,
Advisory Committee on Church Music,
Irish Episcopal Commission for Liturgy.

INDEX OF FIRST LINES

CONTENTS

(a)

Al - le - lu - ia, _____ al - le - lu - ia, al - le - lu - ia, _____
al - le - lu - ia, al - le - lu - ia, _____ al - le - lu - ia,
al - le - lu - ia _____ al - le - lu - ia. VERSE Glo - ry to the Fa - ther,
glo - ry to the Son, glo - ry to the Spi - rit, God the Three-in-One.

(a)
Folk Alleluia
Christopher Walker

Alternative verses:
2
I call you friends because I have told you
everything I've learnt from my Father.
3
Open our hearts, O Lord,
to accept the words of your Son.

(b)

Each two bars sung by Cantor/Choir, then repeated by All

Al - le - lu - ia, al - le - lu - ia. Al - le - lu - ia,
al - le - lu - ia. Al - le - lu - ia, al - le - lu - ia.
Speak, Lord, your servant is listening;
you have the message of e — ter — nal life.

(b)
Alleluia Gaudete
Christopher Walker

Alternative verses:

I bring you news of *great joy:*
today a saviour has been born to us,
Christ the Lord.

May the peace of Christ *reign in your hearts,*
let the message of Christ find a *home with you.*

Your word is *truth, O Lord;*
Consecrate us *in the truth.*

*Any other Gospel verse can be similarly adapted
to this chant.*

177

Alleluia, praise the Lord, all you nations
Fintan O Carroll

2
Proclaim his help day by day,
tell among the nations his glory
and his wonders among all the peoples. *Alleluia.*
3
Bring an off'ring and enter his courts,
worship the Lord in his temple,
O earth, tremble before him. *Alleluia.*
4
Praise the Lord, all you nations,
acclaim him, all you peoples.
Strong is his love for us,
he is faithful forever.

Alleluia sung first by the choir, then repeated by all.

Cantor: Praise the Lord, all you nations,
All: Praise the Lord all you nations,
Cantor: Acclaim him all you peoples!
All: Acclaim him all you peoples!
Strong is his love for us; he is faithful for ever.

Repeat after Cantor first time
Alleluia, alleluia, alleluia, alleluia!

VERSE Cantor
1. O sing a new song to the Lord
Sing to the Lord all the earth. O sing to the Lord, bless his name.
(repeat Alleluia...)

Benedictus Canticle
Ite O'Donovan

178

6
To make known to his people théir sálvátion,
Through forgiveness of áll théir síns.
The loving kindness of the heart óf óur Gód
who visits us like the dáwn fróm ón hígh. R/.

7*
He will give light to thóse ín dárkness,
Those who dwell in the shadów óf déath,
And guide us in tó thé wáy óf péace.

8
Give praise to the Fáther Álmíghty,
to his Son, Jesus Chríst thé Lórd,
to the Spirit, who dwells ín óur héarts,
both now and fór évér, Ámen. R/.

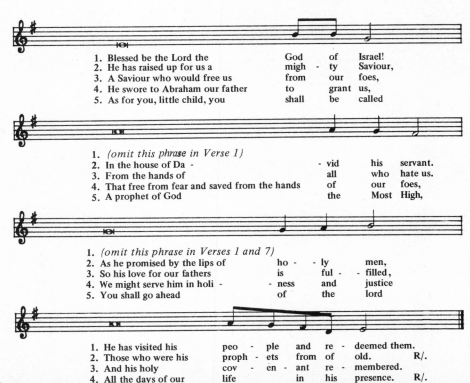

*Omit phrase 3 in this verse

179

Be with me, Lord
Michael Joncas

2
Evil shall never befall you,
nor affliction come near to your tent.
Unto his angels he's given command
to guard you in all your ways.

3
On their hands the angels will bear you up,
lest you dash your foot 'gainst a stone.
Lion or viper might strike at your life,
but you will not come to harm.

Be with me, Lord; be with me, Lord, when I am in trou-ble and
need. ___ *(to verses)* 1. You who dwell in the shel-ter of God, most High, who a-
-bide in Al-migh-ty's shade, ___ say to the Lord: 'My
re-fuge, my strong-hold, my God in whom I trust! ' ___ *(to refrain)*

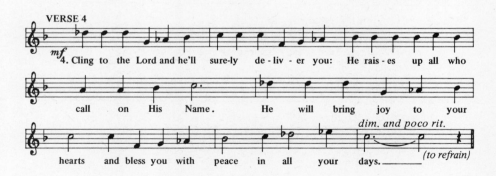

4. Cling to the Lord and he'll sure-ly de-liv-er you: He rais-es up all who
call on His Name. He will bring joy to your
hearts and bless you with peace in all your days. ___ *(to refrain)*

REFRAIN

The hea-vens are tell-ing the glo-ry of God ___ and all cre-a-tion is shouting for joy, ___ come, dance in the for-est, come, play in the field, ___ and sing, sing to the glo-ry of the Lord.

1-5 | **FINAL**

(to verse) Lord. ___ Sing, sing to the glo-ry of the Lord. ___

VERSE

1. Sing to the sun, the bring-er of day, he car-ries the light of the Lord in his rays, the moon and the stars, who light up the way un-to Your throne. ___ *(to refrain)*

2
Praise to the wind that blows through the trees,
the seas mighty storms, the gentlest breeze,
they blow where they will,
they blow where they please
to please the Lord.

3
Praise to the rain that waters our fields
and blesses our crops, so all the earth yeilds,
from death unto life, her myst'ry concealed
springs forth in joy.

4
Praise to the fire who gives us his light,
the warmth of the sun to brighten our night,
he dances with joy, his spirit so bright,
he sings to you.

5
Sing to the earth who makes life to grow,
the creatures you made to let your life show,
the flowers and trees that help us to know
the heart of love.

6
Praise to our death that makes our life real,
the knowledge of loss that helps us to feel
the gift of yourself, your presence revealed
to bring us home.

181

Church of God
Text: Sr Pamela Stotter
Music: Sr Margaret Daly

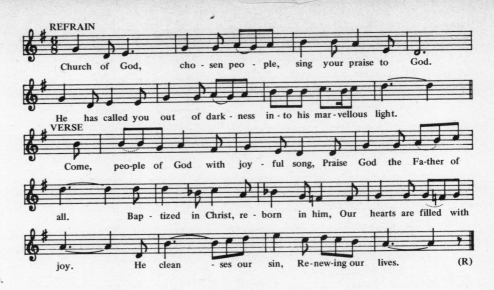

REFRAIN
Church of God, cho-sen peo-ple, sing your praise to God.
He has called you out of dark-ness in-to his mar-vellous light.

VERSE
Come, peo-ple of God with joy-ful song, Praise God the Fa-ther of
all. Bap-tized in Christ, re-born in him, Our hearts are filled with
joy. He clean-ses our sin, Re-new-ing our lives. (R)

2
The Church is built with living stones
with Christ as cornerstone.
In him we trust who makes us one
uniting us in love.
We build on the rock of faith in Christ.

3
As heirs of Christ, redeemed by love,
we wait for his return;
A priestly people off'ring praise
to God, the source of hope.
For Jesus is Lord, our saviour and God.

4
As water springing from the rock
once brought God's people life;
the living water giv'n by Christ
creates our lives anew.
So come, you who thirst, to springs of new hope.

5
May fragrant smoke of incense rise
to fill this house of prayer.
May we who gather find true peace,
God's presence filling our lives.
Our hearts lift with praise, our lips sing in joy.

6
We gather here to worship God,
our Eucharist to share.
We give him thanks and celebrate
the mystery of his love.
The Word is made flesh, and given for us.

7
The light of Christ has come to us
dispelling all our fears.
His light reveals the path of life;
we follow him with joy.
The glory of God, the Light of the world.

♩ = 88

Come to set us free, come to make us your own.

Come to show the way to your peo-ple, your cho-sen.

O - pen our lives to the light of your pro - mise.

Come to our hearts with hea-ling, come to our minds with pow-er,

VERSE

come to us and bring us your life. 1. You are

light which shines in dark-ness, Morn-ing Star which ne - ver sets.

3

O - pen our eyes which on - ly dim - ly

D.C.

see the truth which sets us free.

2
You are hope which brings us courage,
you are strength which never fails.
Open our minds to ways we do not know,
but where your Spirit grows.
3
You are promise of salvation,
you are God in human form.
Bring to our world of emptiness and fear
the word we long to hear.

183

**Eucharistic Acclamations
from the Mass of
St Attracta**
Ite O'Donovan

(a) Pre-Sanctus

With Je-sus we sing your praise: Glory to God, glory to God in the high-est.

(b) Sanctus

Ho-ly, Ho-ly, Ho-ly is the Lord. 1. Ho-ly, Holy, Ho-ly Lord,

God of pow'r and might. R/. 2. Hea - ven and earth are
3. Bless-ed is He who comes in the

full of your glo - ry, Ho - san - na, ho - san - na, ho - san - na in the high - est. R/.
name of the Lord, Ho - san - na, ho - san - na, ho - san - na in the high - est. R/.

(c) Post Consecration

Je-sus has gi-ven his life for us. Je-sus has gi-ven his life for us.

(d) Post Consecration

We praise you, we bless you, we thank you. We praise you, we bless you, we thank you.

(e) Doxology and Great Amen.

Priest: Through Him, with Him, in Him,
All: A - - - - men!

Priest: In the unity of the Holy Spirit.
All: A - - - men!

Priest: All glory and honour is Yours, Almighty Father, for ev - er and ev - er:
All: A - - - - - men!

184

Fógraíonn na spéartha glóire Dé

Ceol: Fiontán Ó Cearrbhaill
Focail: Tadhg Ó Séaghdha

1.Fóg - raíonn na spéar-tha glói - re_ Dé 'S an Oll - chruinn-eacht a _ lámh, Ag_ ló le ló tá'n scéal dhá ríomh is_ oích' le_ h'oích'dhá_ rá. Ní_ clois - tear teang' ar bith dhá labhairt, aon guth_ ná_ friot - al_ béil, Ach_ téigheann an glór a - mach faoin domhan, Go_ críoch na cruin - ne féin.

2
Thóg Dia sa spéir páilliún don ghréin
A éiríos ann gach ló
Amhail nuachar bródúil ó na bhoth
Nó fian chun reatha ag gabháil;
A réim anoir ón áit éirí
Go críoch na spéire thiar,
'S níl éaló ag aon ní ó na bruth
Ná folach ó na brí.

3
Tá dlí an Tiarna fíor gan cháim
Do-ghní aithbhreith 's athnuadh.
Tá reachta an Tiarna dearbh slán
Do-ghní den tsimplí stuaim.
Tá aitheanta an Tiarna ceart
Is tógaid suas an croí;
Tá ordú an Tiarna soiléir beacht
Is léargas súl 'na dhiaidh.

4
Tá adhradh 's eagla an Tiarna glan
Is amhlaidh is dual go bráth.
Tá breithiúnais an Tiarna cóir
Is cothrom fós le cách.
A bhreithiúnais is in-mhéine iad
Ná an t-ór is íne mhín',
Ná blas na meala is milse iad
Ná an mhil is milse ón gcír.

5
Do ghiolla, a bheir dá aire iad—
'S is mór an luaíocht dó:
Ach liacht a locht do neach ní léir—
Ar m'ainriocht folaigh, fóir!
Ar pheaca mór an uabhair fós
Do ghiolla cumhdaigh slán;
Ná mealladh cluain ná daor-chathú
Mo dhílse uait go bráth.

6
Gach briathar liom is smaoineadh bíodh
Gan marach os do chomhair.
Mo dhídean slán thú i chuile ghábh
Mo dhaingean, m'fhuasgaltóir.
(faoi dhó)

Hail, Ma - ry, daughter of God the Fa - ther; Hail, Ma - ry,

Mo-ther of God the Son; Hail, Ma - ry, Spouse of God the Ho - ly

Spi - rit; Hail, Ma - ry, tem - ple of the Most Ho - ly Tri - ni -

- ty. Glo - ry to God the Fa-ther who chose you. Glo - ry to God the Son who

loved you. Glo - ry to God the Ho - ly Spi-rit who e - spoused you. O

glo-rious Vir - gin Ma - ry, may we al - ways love and praise you.

186 **Glastonbury Gloria**
Christopher Walker

(a) Repeat after the Cantor or Choir

Glo - ry to God, glo - ry to God in the high - est
peace to his peo - ple on earth.

Glory to God, glory to God in the highest,
Peace to his people, on earth.

Lord God, heavenly king,
almighty God and Father.

Glory to God . . .

We worship you, give you thanks,
we praise you for your glory.

Glory to God . . .

Lord Jesus Christ, only Son of the Father
Lord God, Lamb of God.

Glory to God . . .

You take away the sins of the world:

Have mer - cy, mer - cy on us,

Have mercy, mercy on us.
You are seated at the right of the Father:

re - ceive our prayer,

Receive our prayer.
Glory to God . . .
Glory to God . . .

Glastonbury Gloria
Christopher Walker

Choir For you a-lone are the Ho-ly One: *All* Glo-ry to God. *Choir* You a-lone are the Lord:

All Glo-ry to God. *Choir* You a-lone are Most High: *All* Glo-ry to God.

Jesus Christ, with the Holy Spirit,
in the glory of God the Father.
Glory to God . . .
Glory to God . . .

Repeat each phrase

A———men, a———men. A———men, a———men.

A———men, a———men. A———men, a - men.

186

Glastonbury Eucharistic Acclamations
Christopher Walker

(b)

Repeat each phrase

Ho - ly, ho - ly, ho - ly Lord,

God of pow - er, God of might, heaven and earth are full of your glo - ry.

Ho - san - na in the high - est. Bles - sed bles - sed is he,

he who comes in the Lord's name. Ho - san - na in the high - est,

ho - san - na in the high - est, ho - san - na!

(c) (d)

Repeat each phrase

Christ _____ has died,
A _____ men,

Christ ____ is ris - en ____ Christ will come a - gain!
A _____ men, ____ m A _____ men!

Is Naofa Thú
Shane Brennan

Is nao - fa, nao - fa, nao - fa

thú. A Thiar - na Dia na Slua.

Cantor *(freely)*

1. Tá neamh agus talamh   lán de do   ghlóir.
2. Is beannaithe an Té 'tá ag teacht in   ainm an   Tiarna.

Cantor   *All*

a tempo Hó - - san - na 'sna h-ar - da.   Hó - - san - na 'sna h-ar - da. Is

(after Verse 2, end at Fine.)

188

Let all the peoples praise you, O Lord

Christopher Willcock, SJ

2
Let this be written for ages to come:
peoples unborn may praise the Lord.
He has come down from his sanctuary on high
to set the prisoners free, Alleluia!

3
Sons of your servants shall dwell untroubled,
and their race shall last for ever.
Let them proclaim the name of the Lord.
We shall worship him: Alleluia!

Let all the peo - ples praise you, O Lord, let all the peo - ples praise you. Let all the peo - ples praise you, O Lord, let all the peo - ples praise you.

VERSE *Cantor*

1. Na - tions shall fear the name of the Lord, and all the kings of earth your glo - ry, when the Lord shall build Si - on a - gain, in all his glo - ry, Al - le - lu - ia!

VERSE Solo

Lord, you have blessed the earth, which wait-ed for your word, turn-ing a des-ert, a land un-sown in-to a gar-den of de-light.

Choir

The glo-ry of Le-ba-non is gi-ven to it; the splen-dour of Car-mel and Sha-ron.

Solo

In Ma-ry our earth has yield-ed fruit and brought forth bread to give us strength, rich in de-light of ev'-ry kind, the bread of e-ter-nal life.

REFRAIN All

The poor shall eat and have their fill and cry out in praise of the Lord; all who were thirs-ty con-tent-ed now, the hun-gry filled with all good.

Lord, you have blessed the earth
Sr Margaret Daly

189

2
Lord, you have blessed the land
your vineyard planted with care;
fragrant its blossoms, abundant its fruit,
Israel's glory and pride.
The glory of Lebanon is given to it
the splendour of Carmel and Sharon.
In Mary the land has yielded fruit:
grapes to be crushed through pain and death,
wine to gladden the human heart,
the cup of eternal life. *(Refrain.)*

3
Lord, you have blessed the world,
the field where you sowed good seed;
white with the promise of harvest already,
the land stands deep in wheat.
The glory of Lebanon is given to it,
the splendour of Carmel and Sharon.
For Mary brought forth the grain of wheat,
which fell to the earth a single grain,
and yielded the harvest of God's elect,
called to eternal life. *(Refrain.)*

190

Our Father (a)
David Saint

Our Fa - ther, who art in Hea - ven, hal - lowed be thy name. Thy King-dom come, thy will be done on earth as it is in heav'n. Give us this day our dai - ly bread and for - give us our tres - pass-es as we for - give those who tres - pass a - gainst us. And lead us not in - to temp - ta - tion, but de - liv - er us from ev - il.

For the King - dom, the power and the glo - ry are yours, now and for - ev - er.

(b)

Lamb of God
David Saint

190

Optional choir verses (for use between the petitions when a longer fraction rite is required)

Choir:
When Jesus was at table with them,
he took the bread and blessed and broke it,
and gave it to them.
2
Their eyes were opened and they recognised him,
they recognised him in the breaking of bread.

191

Path of Life
John Scalea

2
My heart is glad and my soul rejoices.
My body abides in your goodness, O Lord.
I know you're beside me through all of my days.
With you at my right hand I'll not be afraid.

REFRAIN

Lord you show us the path of life: full-ness of joy in your pres-ence for-ev-er; de-lights at your right hand out-last-ing all time. Lord, you show us the path of life. (2. My) life. Lord you show us the path of life. VERSE

1. Keep me, O Lord, for in you I take ref-uge. You are my God: with-out you I'm lost. You help me to cher-ish your peo-ple on earth. And prom-ise a king-dom of won-der and love. *(to refrain)*

Intro/Interlude

REFRAIN: *First time Cantor, then All*

Re - mem-ber, re-mem-ber your mer - cy, Lord.— Re -

- mem-ber, re-mem-ber your mer - cy, Lord.— Hear your people's prayer as they

call to you: re - mem-ber, re-mem-ber your mer - cy, Lord. *Repeat refrain 1st time only*

to Verses VERSE

mer - cy Lord.— (2. Re -) 1. Lord, make me know your ways.

Lord, teach me your paths. Make me walk in your truth, and

teach me: for you are God my Sav - iour.

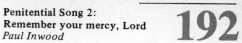

Penitential Song 2:
Remember your mercy, Lord
Paul Inwood

192

2
Remember your mercy, Lord,
and the love you have shown from of old.
Do not remember the sins of my youth.
In your love remember me,
in your love remember me because of your
goodness, O Lord.
(to interlude and response)
3
The Lord is good and upright.
He shows the path to all who stray,
he guides the humble in the right path;
he teaches his way to the poor.
(to interlude and response)

193

Rejoice
Sr Aideen O'Sullivan

REFRAIN 1

This is the day the Lord has made, let us be glad and re-joice in it.

REFRAIN 2

Give thanks to the Lord for he is good, his___ love en-dures for ev - er.

1. Let the sons of Is - rael say:"His___ love en-dures for-
2. Let the sons of Aa-ron say:"His___ love en-dures for-

ev - er." The Lord's right hand has triumphed, his
ev - er."

right hand raised me up. *(refrain 2)* 3. Al - le-lu-ia, I shall not die, I shall

(refrain 2)
live and re-count his deeds. 4. The stone which the build-ers re-

(refrain 1&2)
- jec-ted has proved to be the cor-ner-stone. 5. This is the work of the

Lord, a mar-vel in our eyes, Al-le-lu-

(refrain 1&2)
- ia, his___ love en-dures for ev - er.

CURFA ♩=66

Pád-raig As-pal, al-le-lu-ia, ca-nai-mís le___ dó-chas chroí

BHÉARSA

Éist go fóill le___ glór do mhuintir, 's bí in éin-eacht linn de shíor. 1. Tá

rian na Naomh ar thír na hÉir-eann, rian geal Phád-raig, sois-céal Dé.

Buíoch___ sin-ne,___ muin-tir___ Phád-raig; lean-ai-mís i___ gcón-aí é.

Chorus

Rian Phádraig
Ceol: Pat Ahern
Focail: Oilibhéar Ó Croiligh
Translation: Dermod McCarthy

2 *Chorus*
Rian na gcos ar chruach is díseart,
cill is clog i ndiaidh a shiúil;
Rian an té bhí creagach dílis,
seirbhíseach Rí an nDúl.

3 *Chorus* ①
Rian na mbriathar tá i scríbhinn,
ó Cheannannas Mór go hOileán Í.
Briathar Dé do riar a shaothar:
Déanam beart dá réir arís.

4
Rian an ghrá go buan san Eaglais,
ainneoin peacaí, pian is crá;
Briathar misnigh dúinn ó Phádraig:
'Déanfaidh sibhse fós níos fearr.'

English translation

Chorus:
Pádraig, Aspal, Alleluia!
Sing, while hearts with hope we fill.
Listen to your people calling:
'Come and walk among us still.'

1
See, across the land of Ireland,
signs of Patrick, God's Good News.
We are thankful, we are Patrick's people,
let us follow in the path he chose.

2
Footprints etched on plain and hillside,
Church and bell mark where he trod;
signs which tell us of his strength and fidelity,
tireless worker in the fields of God.

3
Words from scripture stand in witness
from Kells to far Iona's shore;
The Word of God, his word of wisdom:
by it, let us live once more.

4
The mark of love remains among us,
in spite of anguish, pain and sin;
we find hope in the words of Patrick:
'You will do even greater things.'

194

195

**Song of welcome
for the Word**
Christopher Walker

Sing prai-ses to the Lord, Al - le - lu - ia, sing
praise to greet his word: Al - le - lu - ia. His word is a sign of his
wis - dom and his love: Al - le - lu - ia, Al - le - lu - ia.

2
His truth can set us free, **Alleluia!**
Christ Jesus is the key, **Alleluia!**
Our ears hear his word but it
lives within our hearts, **Alleluia! Alleluia!**

3
We listen for his voice, **Alleluia!**
We praise him and rejoice, **Alleluia!**
His Spirit is with us,
It breathes within his word, **Alleluia! Alleluia!**

4
Sing praises to the Lord, **Alleluia!**
Sing praise to greet his word, **Alleluia!**
The Father, the Son and the
Spirit be adored, **Alleluia! Alleluia!**

(a) Ostinato Response

Eat this bread, drink this cup, come to me and nev-er be hun-gry. Eat this bread, drink this cup trust in me and you will not thirst.

(b) Ostinato

Je-sus, re-mem-ber me when you come in-to your King-dom. Je-sus, re-mem-ber me when you come in-to your King-dom.

(c) Ostinato

O Lord hear my pray'r, O Lord hear my pray'r: when I call an-swer me. O Lord hear my pray'r, O Lord hear my pray'r: come and lis-ten to me.

Fine

Stay with me
Remain here with me
Watch & pray
Watch & pray

197 Tar anuas, a Spioraid Naoimh
Ite O'Donovan

2
Sampla na bhfíréan go leanaimid
agus i dTeampall Chríosta go bhfanaimid.

3
Cuid duine eile nár shantaímid,
agus cumann gach duine go gcumhdaímid.

REFRAIN

Tar a - nuas a Spior - aid Naoimh, tar a -
- nuas a Spior - aid Naoimh, tar a - nuas a Spior - aid
Naoimh is líon ár gcroí ded' ghrás - ta caomh.

VERSE

1. Grás - ta an Spior - aid Naoimh go ngabh - a - imid a - gus
in - sa chreid - eamh fíor go gcón - a - ímid. I ngaol
Dé, i ngrá Dé, i dtoil Dé, i súil
poco rall.
Dé, i rún Dé, i gcúr - am Dé.

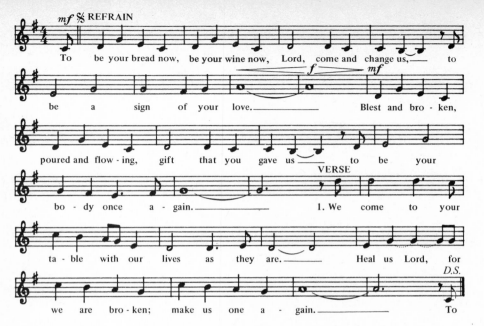

To be your bread
David Haas

2
Lord, we stumble through the darkness of night.
Lead us, now, O Lord, we follow;
bring us home to you.
3
Give us the bread and wine that bring us to life;
feed us, and we'll never hunger,
never thirst again.

REFRAIN

To be your bread now, be your wine now, Lord, come and change us, to be a sign of your love. Blest and broken, poured and flow-ing, gift that you gave us to be your bo-dy once a-gain.

VERSE

1. We come to your ta-ble with our lives as they are. Heal us Lord, for we are bro-ken; make us one a-gain. To

199

We have been told
David Haas

2
'You are my friends, if you keep my commands,
no longer slaves, I call you friends.'
3
'No greater love is there than this:
to lay down one's life for a friend'.

REFRAIN

We have been told, we've seen his face, and heard his voice a - live in our hearts; 'Live in my love with all your heart, as the Fa - ther had loved me, so

1 + 2

I have loved you.'

Final - after V.3

I have loved you; As the Fa - ther has loved me, so I have loved you.

VERSE

1. 'I am the vine, you are the branch - es, and all who live in me will bear great fruit.'